MUSINGS

SUDHIR MENON

Made with ♥ on the Notion Press Platform
www.notionpress.com

This book is dedicated to the multitude of people who have crossed my path in life and my interactions with them and to life itself for having given me this humongous exposure to reflect on its several aspects, which may seem to be commonplace but are in themselves weighty concepts, and evolve meaningful conclusions which, hopefully, would prove to be inspirational to the reader.

Contents

Contents

Disclaimer

All the characters in the various articles included in this book and the events related thereto are fictional and have no bearing to any person living or dead. Any resemblance of a character to any person or the association of a situation to an event, past or present, is purely coincidental.

Other titles by the same author :

1)A Ghastly Trail
2)Curry Leaf
3)Third Factor
4)Passing Clouds and other tales
5)Winsome Days and other tales
6)Relationships
7)No One Runs Forever

ONE

Impact of Language

Language has always been the basis of mass communication. The proclivity of peoples and whole populations to coalesce and merge into a cohesive whole, lies to a major extent on the ability to communicate through a common language. It is the unseen force that binds commoners and kings, the populace and governments alike.

It is, therefore, a major factor in one's personality which endears the person to everyone that he or she comes in contact with. Without the proficiency in at least one language, a person would find his or her communication is stifled, progress is stunted - nay, even life's journey is bereft of joy and understanding.

Language, therefore being a medium of communication, strikes at the very heart of human relationships and is the hallmark of creating understanding or misunderstanding between two or more individuals, groups or even nations.

This brings me to the important aspect of how language is conveyed. In terms of the spoken word, language has to be simple, mild, clear and concise for it to be effective in communication. There cannot be a worse situation than when something is spoken in a harsh or speedy manner such that the person or persons to whom it is addressed is left more confused than before. Since the spoken word is often conveyed on the spur of the moment, care must be taken to ensure that the language is congenial and acceptable to avoid the possibility of regrets being felt by the person at a later stage. The spoken word, therefore, is like water which has flowed from the tap which cannot be retrieved. Having said that, often a certain leniency is extended for the spoken word in terms of accepting its legitimacy as it is governed by the individual's frame of mind at that point in time.

On the other hand, the written word is often considered to be the writer's last word on the subject he or she has written. It may not be so, for an individual's thought process is dynamic based on external factors that may influence the person's perception, but, nevertheless, it is an unwritten fact that is accepted by the vast majority of people that when somebody has written something, the individual had applied his or her mind to the subject. In such a case, therefore, the written word is a more serious and deliberate manifestation of communication of a subject. Often, a written statement or passage is the culmination of a series of efforts or drafts, each successive attempt being an improvement or edited version of the earlier one. That being the case, it would be in order to highlight the importance of vocabulary in language. Mark Twain had once remarked, 'the difference between the almost right word and the right word is really a large matter - tis the difference between the lightning bug and the lightning'. His words are so apt and the analogy he has employed drives home the point in all the intensity that was intended. It is the right word that creates the impact on the reader's mind about the matter that is being conveyed by the writer. If chosen wisely by the writer, there will not be a better word to substitute the one which had been selected. It is the pursuit of achieving excellence in this skill that hones a beginner into becoming a seasoned writer. The 'right' word does not necessarily imply that the word has to be bombastic or complicated. Even a simple word can create the intended impact for the text in question.

A point which relates to the right word is the art of being brief in what one has to say. William Shakespeare had occasion to say, 'brevity is the soul of wit' (in the play Hamlet - Act 2 Scene 2). Nothing could be further than the truth. While the right word brings along with it a whole lot of imagery to convey the point in question, it is the foundation for being brief in communicating an idea. Such is the impact of language if it is spoken or written in the appropriate manner.

TWO

ART OF COMMUNICATION

What's the use of knowing a language if one cannot communicate with it? In an earlier dispatch, I had dwelt on the 'impact of language' as a medium of communication. This week, I shall touch upon three aspects in the art of communication which are paramount for it to be fructuous.

First of all, in order that communication is effective, the message that is conveyed should be received and understood by the receiver *in the manner that the sender intended it to be.* It is necessary, therefore, to appreciate the fact that by just speaking in an audible voice or sending across a letter or other missive, one does not effectively 'communicate' to the other party, unless there is a presence, both physical and mental, of the other party of being aware of what is being spoken and the tenor of the conversation.

Having said that, it is mandatory for a person who wishes to communicate to ensure that the other party *is ready to receive the communication.* It would be foolish on the part of the communicator to try and make the other party understand what he is saying without first assessing the mood, availability and readiness to receive the communication. If one should go ahead without having clarity on these three parameters, it would be tantamount to infringement on the other party's space without any effect, which could also cause misunderstanding, friction and unnecessary upheaval.

Consequent to what has been said hitherto, it would be reasonable to assume that the receiver of communication must be *ready to listen and not just hear.* The subtle difference between 'hearing' and 'listening' is that while one is related to 'perception', the other is principally a pre-requisite for 'cognition'. This means that 'listening' is not only perception but includes attentiveness, reasoning and memory recall. Listening, therefore, is an art of consciously being aware of what is being communicated by living in the present moment without any fetters mentally.

In conclusion, therefore, it would be pertinent to state that there should be an unseen attachment between the sender and receiver of communication such that it results in a perfect understanding leading to clarity of action wherever required. In today's world, the future holds good for those who can effectively communicate and the art of communication will continue to be the torch-bearer for peoples and nations in demolishing geographical, religious, caste, creed, communal and language boundaries so as to build a more cohesive world for future generations.

THREE

The Habit of Reading

How often have we heard people say, 'I don't have the time to read', 'I am not into reading', 'Reading is definitely not my passion', or 'I can never sit down to read'. This phenomenon is not surprising in today's digital world, where people find a preponderance of diverting their faculties towards the satiation of their inclinations in cyber space. True, that the 'messages' sent back and forth would be communicative and often interesting; but, is the essential requirement in one's life of laying hands on researched and creative literature even being skimmed on the periphery?

'Certainly not', a high priest for the propagation of 'literature' would say. For 'reading' besides providing knowledge and entertainment must necessarily enrich the mind on a continuous course of self-improvement. Sir Francis Bacon (1561 – 1626), the great English philosopher, empiricist and father of the scientific revolution had once said, 'reading maketh a full man ...'. He envisioned that reading should be imbibed by every human being in their daily lives such that they feel exalted by its influence.

Reading expands vocabulary, boosts memory, develops analytical and communication skills and directs the mind to be focused. It brings in its wake, a reservoir of knowledge and experience that transports the reader to the time and situations that are enunciated between the covers of a book. It often causes the reader to relate to similar situations in his or her own life and may suggest solutions for existing or impending problems. It exults the reader in the appreciation of a brilliant climax and expands the fringes of the mind to the acceptance of renewed possibilities.

Reading is not only good for the intellect but also for health. Research has shown that reading reduces muscle tension and slows the heartbeat besides fostering decision-making. As compared to listening to music, drinking tea, walking or playing video games, reading reduces stress and the risk of incidental dementia by a greater extent.

However, cautions Francis Bacon, 'read not to contradict and confute; nor to believe and take for granted; nor to find talk and discourse; but to *weigh* and *consider*'. Reading, therefore, must leverage the mind and intellect to higher levels of thought and appreciation resulting in a wider perspective of life and its multifarious issues. It must provide a platform that induces the reader to reflect and surmise on the subject matter in a dispassionate and logical manner.

On the subject of widening our horizons, Francis Bacon had this to say, 'the universe must not be narrowed down to the limit of our understanding, but our understanding must be stretched and enlarged to take in the image of the universe as it is discovered'. Falling in line with this sensible and wise advice, the human race would do well to ingrain the rudiments of the habit of reading in their respective lives.

FOUR

SCOURGE OF EXPECTATION

'I am expecting a promotion' is a commonly-heard sentiment expressed in a company where merit is recognized. 'I expect him to call me and discuss the matter', is another expression echoed by many in their daily lives. These are just examples of how the feeling of 'expectation' influences our lives and consequently our emotions, happiness and relationships.

'Expectation' in any form, where the fruition of one's actions is dependent on the perception of another, is a recipe for disappointment. Often, one does not see the manifestation of one's expectations because the person from whom something is expected does not perceive the subject matter in question in the manner that was expected to be perceived. Again, an action which is expected to happen may not take place for a variety of intervening factors. In both these cases, too much reliance on one's expectation for something to fructify is a non-starter and an exercise in foolhardiness, ultimately giving way for disappointment to set in. As Sylvia Plath, the acclaimed

American poet and writer, states, 'If you expect nothing from somebody you are never disappointed'.

Having said that, one should keep one's expectations high wherever one has a full control of one's actions, e.g. preparing for an exam, participation in a tournament, driving a car with a sober temperament are all instances of one's calibre and self-initiative at play. These are all actions which may warrant a feeling of hope of success in the venture. The moment there is the influence of another individual in one's journey to success, the latter may slip into domain of expectancy which must be avoided. Keeping one's expectation high on achievement and low on people will prevent one from falling into the morass of disappointment leading to frustration and unhappiness.

This does not mean that one should give up 'hope' of being appreciated or of the happening of a certain event, for human beings by nature would wish to wait and absorb the consequence of their actions; and, if it were to be in the same strain of thought, one can possibly go gung-ho over it. But that's as far as hope may be stretched; else one can get a load of frustration in the realm of expectation. So, one must cultivate the regimen of 'always hoping but never expecting'.

Another important aspect of expectation is that it rears its ugly head in relationships where one individual is attached to another, e.g. in the case of a husband and wife, two relatives or even two friends. This is because in such close relationships, there is a tendency for taking each other for granted without even leaving an iota of thought or credence to the fact that human beings are different and will react differently at different times. Such blind attachment to one another can, therefore, lead to unrealistic expectations and would become a source of suffering.

An interesting sidelight presents itself in the corporate world where the management must assess the expectations of employees because in so doing, they would be able to fulfil and probably even exceed the latter's hopes and aspirations. When this happens, the employees would consistently exceed the expectations of the customers which brings us to the well-known corporate mantra, 'if the employees are happy, they'll take care of the customers who in turn will then take care of the business of the company'.

In conclusion, therefore, it may be said that expectation is a weakness which one may easily succumb to which could cloud one's happiness in the journey through life and the ideal way to counter this temptation is to perform the duties to the best of one's abilities and not bother about the fruits of such actions.

FIVE

Taking a Stand

The other day, a friend of mine was in a spot – he'd been hoodwinked into participating in a live painting competition and though he was a master with the brush, his magnificent and colourful effort did not evince interest nor find favour with the panel of judges, who awarded the winning prize for a painting which would not as much as have received a second glance from anyone who would have had the right understanding of the rudiments of the art. My friend was crestfallen. He clearly felt cheated. The competition had ended in a joke. Even the connoisseurs with their ever-probing eagle eyes, who would invariably have been able to sift between the chaff and the grain, were shell-shocked when the final result was announced.

But my friend stood his ground. After the brouhaha amongst the discerning audience had died down and the curtains came down over the event, he shot off a missive to the organizers of the competition detailing the use of pedestrian parameters by the judging panel in deciding the winner. For sure, this must have come like a bolt from the blue for the organizers, who were resting content with the fact that their shady decision had not been questioned by anyone. For shady it was, as the winner was the nephew of a patron of the institution which had conducted the competition. How dare my friend find fault with their judgement, was the one thought that pervaded the sick minds of the organizers and the judging panel. Brushing aside all norms of decency and decorum, my friend was suspended from the membership of the all-powerful 'National Painters' Association' and debarred from participation in competitions and expositions for a period of five years. As destiny would have it, my friend accepted the decision in his stride and soon projected it as a blessing in disguise; for he and like-minded flourishing maestros broke away from the debauched association, after the truth of the competition result was revealed, and formed their own collective to promote the art in its right perspective.

This brings me to the crux of the issue – taking a stand. My friend did not dither in his self-confidence but took up cudgels to remonstrate and expose to the world at large, the infamy behind a much-touted competition. He took a stand even at the risk of being ostracized by others in his profession, because he felt that being taken for a ride was not part of his regimen. He had the gumption to do so and he did it with elan and with a feeling of rectitude.

So, what does 'taking a stand' do to an individual. Initially it may deprive him of his current status since the 'adversary' would be an establishment or an institution or someone in the corridors of power. Then, he would, in all probability, be subjected to criticism by peers and seniors alike, as the acknowledged belief in all such cases is that the individual is throwing his weight around and unnecessarily rocking his own boat. These feelings gain ground from the fact that most people on this planet would like to remain within their own circle of comfort and sticking one's neck out, even if it is an attempt to redress a wrong is a strict no-no. In India, we term this as the '*chalta hai*' attitude.

However, not everyone would react abruptly or adversely to the lone ranger. For several individuals worth their salt, a person who takes a stand on a controversial matter affecting him, with a mission to expose the truth, stands tall in the annals of living a life with dignity and courage. He is often looked upon as the messiah who took a stand so that a message could flow from his action for others to follow. He would become an instant hero and a torchbearer for several others languishing in similar situations around the globe. In this regard, it is pertinent to quote the oft repeated saying, 'if you don't stand for something, you will fall for anything'.

But in order to take a stand, an individual needs to have the moral high ground as his integrity is paramount in exposing a murky situation; and in this exercise, he will ultimately feel a sense of achievement for, besides having a clear conscience, he would have convincingly cleared the air.

SIX

EMPOWERMENT IS KEY

Sakharam was in the doldrums. A poor daily wage-earner, he had lost his measly job because of the downturn in the real estate sector. Not that he was not capable of another employment, for he had studied up to the eighth standard, but the market was flush with unemployed people more qualified than him. Sakharam was also quite willing to accept any another job, should one come his way; but, as fate would have it, he was destined to wallow in penury. Sakharam's predicament is not unique in our society. Millions like him have to eke out a living on a daily basis.

This brings me to the crux of the core problem in our vast country – that of unemployment giving way to impoverishment. As of Dec. 2021, 53 million were unemployed in India (as per the Centre for Monitoring Indian Economy) and 80 million people in 2019 were below poverty line of $1.25 (as per UN Millennium Development Goals programme). These figures would have definitely increased as on date and the picture become gloomier.

Given a choice, would our poor citizens be willing to dwell in their small world of doom? Certainly not. For, since the beginning of mankind, the greatest existential driving force for man has been the search for a durable source for satiating his hungry belly. Having satisfied his hunger, he would be in an advantageous position to think and strategize logically.

So, what is it that needs to be done to provide the wherewithal to our teeming millions of poor and unemployed people to rise above the morass that they find themselves in? Certainly not a dole of three or fewer meals per day by well-meaning NGOs or others with a zeal to alleviate the sufferings of the marginalized. No, that is not a permanent solution. Besides, it would only cause the poor to further slide into the chasm of being vulnerable to even more retrograde issues affecting their perspective. For instance, they may feel that since food is easy to come by, they needn't work causing them to be a lethargic lot. The need of the hour, therefore, is to ***empower them toearn their livelihood;*** and this is achieved only by a ***massivetwo-pronged initiative – imparting education and developing skills.***

Every individual comes into this world with a certain talent and skill-set endowed by the Almighty, just as we know that every child comes into this world with the message that God is not yet tired of man. Even so, it is left to the individual to assess his strengths and in the case of an impoverished, unemployed person this is well-nigh impossible because the struggle to survive on a daily basis, knocks off all thoughts of self-assessment and improvement, if any, from the mind of such an individual. In this scenario, therefore, these unfortunate individuals live their entire lives without knowing or even having an opportunity to reflect on their strengths, for their only aim, and rightfully so, is to ensure their next meal on the table for themselves and their families. Let us, for a moment, pause and contemplate on this enormous loss of resources, of wasted talent and skills which could have been put to good use for the betterment of the nation. For apart from trying to secure three meals a day, the underprivileged and the unemployed at the very bottom of the pyramid have no other aim in life. This is a dangerous situation for as V. I. Lenin once said, 'Every society is three meals away from chaos'.

So, how can we harness this enormous reservoir of talent and skill? This is an initiative which must be taken up on a *war footing* by the government in power. They have to mobilize all the resources at their command to create schools for imparting education and developing skills from the most under-developed village in the country to the urban environment. A great deal of organizational capability would be required to goad like-minded individuals and voluntary organizations like NGOs, etc. to veer round for this laudable national mission with a single-minded vision of nationalism and patriotism, such that over a period of a decade or so, whole clusters of the population would have been enriched with regular education or skill development or both.

Why is this so important? Because a person excels in a task which he executes passionately and with full cognizance of the fact that he is enjoying every bit of it. And what better way can he have of earning a decent livelihood, because when put to a test, every minute of the hour he'll give out his best.

The deciding factor for this gargantuan national task, however, is the will to push the envelope. Nothing moves on the ground unless there is a dogged determination and will to ensure success. And the success in this case, cannot be measured by sporadic spurts of exultation from various corners of the country, but has to be a journey, a movement of unending proportions to lift the livelihoods of whole sections of the population to a new era of contentment and hope.

SEVEN

'NEED TO KNOW' POLICY

How often have we heard somebody say, 'You don't need to know this', 'This is not for you to know' or 'If it's necessary for you to know, I'll tell you'. These are all emphatic statements made by one person to another with the sole purpose of inhibiting the latter's natural tendency to be intrusive. However, is being intrusive, as a personality trait, a negative quality? It's definitely not so, where it involves acquiring information on matters of one's interest or where one is intrinsically intertwined in a particular situation or subject. For instance, if one is ordering food from restaurants on a regular basis, it is often required to be intrusive to know what the ingredients of the cooked food are, for example, the cooking medium used. Even reviews from customers need to be read to appreciate customer experience. Similarly, if one is going to be administered an injection in a hospital, it is well worth being aware that a new syringe and needle is utilised for the purpose. Nowadays, with all the downturn in the economy and the escalation in costs, it would not be unbecoming to believe that all sorts of adulteration and shady practices are in vogue. In all such cases, it would be foolish if one is not alert and prudent to thwart the incidence of malpractices from affecting one's well-being and health. So, what have we here? A feeling of consensus that being intrusive in all cases where external factors or situations have a direct bearing on the health, safety and security of an individual is pertinent and in fact wise.

'Curiosity kills the cat' is an adage we have heard from time immemorial and will continue to hear for ages to come. This refers to the negative aspect of curiosity and should not be confused with the positive side of inquisitiveness motivated, for example, by scientific temper which a genius must possess to bring about great advances in science and engineering. How true, therefore, that intrusiveness for the sake of curiosity alone is not only annoying but may also put the individual in harm's way. For instance, a quarrel between two people on the thoroughfare is an instance where one's intrusiveness, if any, is solely engineered by curiosity. Again, intruding into one's privacy by peering into the neighbour's home when the door is open, is another common example of intrusiveness being motivated by curiosity. In these, as in all similar cases, an individual indulging in such delinquent actions would subject himself to unnecessary harm and annoyance. Also, when an individual tries to pry on matters which have no bearing on his life, he would only be inviting needless wrath and criticism from people around him.

This, therefore, brings us to the crux of the issue which makes intrusiveness a bane in the lives of others. It is because some people never really get interested in something, until they realize it is none of their business. With an erroneous feeling of nothing to lose and everything to gain, people do indulge in intrusiveness as a way of life, until they are rebuked and reprimanded in good measure at which juncture, they may slink away unabashedly only to surface at another location and situation to further whet their surging tide of curiosity. It is best to avoid such persons in society. As Horace, the famous Roman poet once said, 'Avoid inquisitive persons, for they are sure to be gossips, their ears are open to hear, but they will not keep what is entrusted to them'.

It is interesting, however, to understand why some people behave in this manner. More often than not, such individuals wish to be the first source of all information in their neighbourhood and the constant endeavour to be at the right time and in the right place, in order to be able to do so, is so overpowering that these individuals would consciously not waste an opportunity to garner 'information'. There is nothing wrong, however, with this posture if one is a journalist or reporter for a newspaper or magazine. In such a case, it would be considered to be a superlative feat of being the first respondent to a particular situation and in the journalistic profession, such initiatives are laudable and are looked upon with utmost reverence. But, in all other cases, unnecessary indulgence in a disrespectful pursuit of 'information' is looked down upon and never encouraged.

This brings me to the topic that I was trying to highlight which is the 'need-to-know policy' in our interactions with others in our daily lives. This policy simply expounded refers to an individual requiring to know only those pieces of information which have a direct bearing on his life and interests. Any other matter is considered to be redundant and hence the individual is not expected to go in pursuit of gleaning details of the same or directly confront others to be apprised of such information. Consequently, this policy requires a great deal of discretion and exercise of decency and decorum. Adhering to this policy, not only maintains an individual's mind at peace and harmony for 'ignorance is bliss', but also guarantees him with a reputation as one who 'minds his own business'.

EIGHT

LIVING IN THE PAST

As Soman glances at the long shadows behind him cast by the setting sun, he becomes conscious of the passing of another day and getting a trifle closer to his twilight years. He has had been a relative success in his field of professional endeavour and now is in the process of evolving a strategy for a lifestyle after the lapse of his productive years. Would it be to follow his passion or do the things he had always wanted to do but could not find the time to do it in? He does not know at this moment but move ahead, he shall, in life in order to maintain his physical health and his grey cells active.

Soman is one of those progressive individuals who has always wanted to move on ahead in life. It is true that he has had a splendid career, but he has never dwelt on the episodes of success along the that may have caused him to digress from his chosen path of activity. It is indeed heartening to note that today there are several men of substance in our society who prefer to push forward with some initiative, calling or pastime rather than wallow in the glory of their illustrious past.

This, in fact, is the cornerstone of finding peace and satisfaction with oneself of having lived a full life in a manner that was conducive in the available circumstances. As Debashish Mridha, the eminent neurologist, philosopher, poet-seer and author so aptly pronounces, 'Procrastination is a way of living in the past instead of the present moment'. When we live in the past, we tend to delay our work in the present and consequently cause a retarding force to be forming a drag on our daily lives.

That is not to say, however, that we should never reflect on our past years and laurels. However, these should only be a yardstick for future exploits as success is a journey and not a destination. Our lives are dynamic and should not be sequestered by the thoughts, however favourable they may be, of having achieved great heights in the past. As the prolific writer, Marty Rubin avers, 'Memories are a nice place to visit, but a terrible place to live'. In a similar vein, therefore, one should not completely lose sight of the past but use it as a leverage to gain fresh ground in the present and future. For instance, if an individual has been proficient in playing chess in his younger days but could not take his passion to the next level, there is no reason why he should not attempt this in his later life if circumstances permit him to do so. So, while dwelling in the past has got its baneful effects on an individual's life, fleeting memories that had spelt success could definitely provide an impetus for him to proceed with a renewed feeling of self-confidence in his chosen path.

Even so, the past is one phase in an individual's life which cannot be altered and, therefore, living in the present is the best bet for any human being. We often think that we will live for the day and cross the bridges when these arrive in our lives; but, in reality, it is far from the truth. As David Icke, a former footballer and published author, so rightly says, 'We go through our lives thinking we are living in the present when in truth we are living in the past and the future'. The solution for this conundrum is very clear – focus on matters that are material to your lives at the moment. This will provide a cover for any possible hindrances that may be caused by excessive consideration of past actions.

For individuals who have had a past, best forgotten, it would be intrinsically illogical to even go down memory lane. A gloomy past can in no way spur an individual to take risks and succeed, because every time he reflects on his past, he would be involved in an imbroglio which would drag him further into an abyss. Even so, such an individual should gather courage to ensure that he carves out a life in his present and future which is devoid of the suffering that he had endured in his early life. If he is conscious of this, then as Fernando Pessoa in his work 'The Book of Disquiet' states, 'My past is everything I failed to be', he would strive to raise his destiny from the depths of a nadir to the heights of a zenith in the time and with the resources that are available to him.

Even with all the care that an individual may take to ensure that the actions in his present life are not overwhelmed by the memories of his early life, it would be like asking for a miracle to see this through, for as Jayne Castel, the celebrated novelist, writing on medieval historical fiction, states, 'It does not matter how much we distance ourselves, how far we run – the past always shadows us'.

NINE

'STAY THE COURSE'

The other day, I visited my friend, Sandip, in his newly acquired apartment. He was restless and for a good reason – his son, Vikram, who had represented his state in badminton had decided to wrap up and digress into playing tennis. The lad was a novice in tennis and would, in the normal course, have taken quite a while to achieve the heights that he had reached in badminton.

"Why this sudden change in direction?" I asked casually.

"Vikram feels there is more scope in tennis, as the nation has not produced much talent of late," replied Sandip, exuding a picture of frustration and disgust.

I reflected for a moment and then, addressing Sandip, said, "Suggest you tell him to stay the course."

My suggestion seemed to touch a chord in Sandip's mind, and he stood up from his crouched position flourishing a smile of relief. "Will you convince him on this?" he asked.

"Of course, I will, as I always have," I stated categorically. Sandip heaved a sigh of relief.

Many of us face this dilemma in our lives, time and again, of having the temptation to dilute our concentration on what we have been doing and stray into uncharted territory. Although this is by no means a totally foolhardy bent of mind, a ray of success in this venture can be envisaged only if the benefits of such action far outweigh the risks that need to be taken. In the case of Vikram, I felt that he had assiduously reached a level and laid the foundations of a career where he needn't have to look back; and beginning another activity from scratch and succeeding in it was a trifle too risky. Besides, he was ranked No.6 in the country which, by any yardstick, was no mean achievement.

This, therefore, brings me to the point I am making – in life, we need to stay the course when we have achieved a certain level of mastery and recognition in our vocation or calling. Just as a rolling stone gathers no moss, it is imperative that one focuses on his present activity and priorities to maintain fixity of purpose and proficiency in operation so that, over time, he registers a quantum leap in his chosen path. Talking about focus, there is an interesting observation on record to highlight this feature, wherein it has been described as '**F**ollowing **O**ne **C**ourse **U**ntil **S**uccessful'. In doing so, one transforms his life from a position of ordinariness to that of being in the realm of the extraordinary, blazing a trail of instances enshrining a saga of determination, dedication and tenacity. This leads to success along the way and pushes the individual to achieve further goals as they come in sight.

Having said that, it is necessary to accept the fact that the concept of 'staying the course' is not bereft of setbacks and criticism. Every person on the path of his duty will encounter either a distraction or deliberate attempt by an external source to scuttle his endeavours. This is a natural consequence of achieving proficiency in one's line of duty; for it is not in everyone's palate to savour and digest the success achieved by another. Even so, an individual must not react and parry the disillusioning factor in his path with as much as a rebuff; instead, he must steadfastly proceed towards the culmination of his professed goals, for what would he achieve by brooding on an unfortunate attempt at derailment of his path. As a world-renowned beverage company advises its employees to 'stay the course' and perform, rather than not be cowed down by the aggressive tactics of competition, it is imperative that a resolute individual who will not retrace his steps and instead crush the thorns that may be strewn in his path, will stride ahead to reach the pinnacle of success.

As Arjuna, in response to his guru, Dronacharya's query during an archery training session, of what is it that he sees in the water below vis-à-vis the wooden fish that the latter has tied high up on a tree, replies that he sees only the eye of the fish! This is an incredible example of being focused and staying the course. All his brothers and even Karna reveal that they see the reflection of many other things like the sky, the trees and branches and the fish, but it is only Arjuna, the ace-archer, who emphatically states that he only sees the fish's eye. It is only a matter of time thereafter that such dedication begets success.

Winston Churchill had a different take on 'staying the course'. In his words, 'Success is not final; failure is not fatal; it is the courage to continue that counts'. In other words, he emphasized on the strength and resilience of an individual that emanated from within to pursue relentlessly his chosen goal, which could take on any storm that loomed in the horizon.

As Will Rogers, the famous American vaudeville performer once said, 'The road to success is dotted with many tempting parking places', it is necessary that we do not stop and fritter away our energies, strengths and resources but garner the same to 'stay the course' in everything that we have ventured to achieve. So, as we go along in life with a clear direction, let us not falter or rest for want of determination, dedication and perseverance, for it is the tortoise which won the race against the hare for having 'stayed the course'.

TEN

Doing Less but Doing Well

In an earlier article, I had touched upon the subject of focus and 'staying the course'. Today, I shall dwell on a topic which may be considered as a spill-over from that discussion. I shall term it, in short, as the effects of 'multitasking'.

We have all heard the term, 'multitasking'. Among the many definitions of the word, the most apt refers to the 'ability to deal with more than one task at the same time'. This can be applied to a person or a computer or other machinery, but my discussion shall remain limited to the effects of multitasking on a person.

It is common knowledge that several companies and corporations nowadays consider it as a strength on the part of the employee to multitask. Advertisements for openings in these work-places will invariably mention this 'quality' as an essential pre-requisite for being selected for a job. From the point of view of these companies, multitasking is being encouraged because it impacts the bottom-line. Sure enough, with fewer employees performing more tasks, it goes to reduce costs of human resources while stretching the abilities of the employees to the maximum. In short, it moulds the employees into becoming 'jacks of all trades...'; but do they become 'masters of none'? The answer is 'no' because there are several in employment who have mastered the 'skill' of doing several activities simultaneously, more so as a necessity to retain their jobs, without having had the ignominious experience of being admonished by their superiors for faltering somewhere along the way. These are the so-called supermen and superwomen in corporate parlance who tend to climb the hierarchical ladder at a faster pace than their colleagues. They are the trend-setters of the working space where the cruel rat-race to prove one's strengths are put to test.

Having said that, let us travel back in time to understand the basis of the industrial revolution vis-à-vis the utilisation of human resources. It was a considered opinion then that division of labour would bring about specialisation and increase in productivity of employees. Needless to say, the experience worked wonders and soon there were thousands of men and women having acquired specific skills and qualified in various professions ready to take on the challenges that faced the new age. It is going back in history now to reminisce on those bygone days when manufacturing and services progressed in leaps and bounds for the betterment of mankind.

For the vast majority of workers and employees, even now, multitasking is a bane, bringing in its wake enormous insecurity, frustration and stress. This is because, while corporates encourage multitasking at every stage, the people at the helm are ill-equipped or downright sadistic when it comes to allocating various unrelated tasks to their subordinates. Without assessing the abilities of their juniors to perform certain tasks with elan, they prefer to strut around their area of command, delegating jobs to these unfortunate employees without proper training, engagement, nay, even with no accountability. In the process, therefore, the employees, devoid of any expertise to do multifarious tasks simultaneously, falter at every step they take and then, being administered the inevitable rebuke, sulk at their 'incompetence' leading to development of inferiority complexes and sometimes even sinking into depression.

One of the intrinsic characteristics of multitasking is the fact that everything needs to be done 'immediately'. Of course, it is taken for granted that everything has to be done well. In this scenario, there results a lot of dilution in focus and attention and according to Deepak Chopra, the renowned motivational speaker and self-improvement guru, 'Multitasking divides your attention and leads to confusion and weakened focus'.

So, if multitasking has to perforce become the order of the day, what is it that needs to be done to give it a dignified semblance of success? As the eminent modern day management expert, Stephen Covey, states, 'The key is not to prioritise what's on your schedule, but to schedule your priorities'. In short, nothing is achieved by doing several things at once, but in deliberate serial execution after detailed planning. As Jeremy Clarkson, the famous English broadcaster and journalist has said, and rightly so, 'Multitasking is the ability to screw everything up simultaneously'. He refers to the immediacy that is inherent in the concept of multitasking.

There are varying opinions whether human beings are wired to multitask. One of the prominent thinkers and scientists in the field of developmental molecular biology, who has done pioneering work in the development of the human brain, John Medina, states, 'The brain cannot multitask. Multitasking, when it comes to paying attention, is a myth. The brain naturally focuses on concepts sequentially, one at a time...To put it bluntly, research shows that we can't multitask. We are biologically incapable of processing information-rich inputs simultaneously...Studies show that a person who is interrupted takes 50 percent longer to accomplish a task. Not only that, he or she makes up to 50 percent more errors'. These sentiments are echoed by Thibaut, the famous German jurist, when he is categorical in stating that 'Multitasking is the sign of a stressed and diseased mind simultaneously doing many things poorly. Quality work and quality thinking require quiet focus'.

This brings me to the oft-repeated quote of one of my teachers in school. At least twice a week he had occasion to say, '*Bhaley kam karo, par sahi karo*' (you may do less, but do it well). How true, I would think, of not burdening the students to do exercises in physics, chemistry and mathematics all at once in the same period! Since then, I have been a votary of shunning multitasking and attempting to do everything with a sense of precision and, albeit, excellence; for what begets perfection, but a sustained onslaught of excellent execution.

Whatever may the case for multitasking, where numerous scientists, philosophers and thinkers have expressed their views, one must neither forget nor take for granted the multitasking that takes place in one's own home by one's own mother. As Linda Poindexter, the celebrated writer and humorist says, 'There are people in this world who spend every day making important decisions, troubleshooting, refereeing fights, nursing egos, doing damage control and multitasking. They are called mothers'. They are the best example ever of multitasking and everyone's upbringing is dependent to a certain extent on the degree of success that their respective mothers would have achieved in their attempts at multitasking.

ELEVEN

LIVEN UP WITH A LIGHTER MIND

"Shove it in that corner," said Malathy to her husband, Vasudev, referring to her elaborate make-up box, even as the latter grappled with the mounds of clothes that were required to be packed, rather stuffed into a fair-sized suitcase which the couple were carrying on their journey to Jaipur.

"Do you really need the box with all its contents? Could you not make do with only a select few cosmetics, etc.? After all, our trip would last only four days," said Vasudev, with a sidelong look at his wife.

"No, I need to take the entire box with all its contents, so no pruning and no selection," replied Malathy, emphatically.

"Well, okay," said Vasudev in a tone which conveyed a mixture of disgust and helplessness, as he proceeded to repack the contents of the suitcase, to make way for the make-up box. "We may have to take another bag also, a smaller one perhaps."

"If you need to, well why not?"

This is precisely what happens to all of us in our daily lives. We tend to stuff our minds with all sorts of unwanted and superfluous thoughts that invade and ravage it with a sustained frequency. However, unlike packing clothes and other articles for a sojourn, where the availability of additional space in terms of an extra bag is a possibility, the mind becomes convoluted with the infringement of unnecessary thoughts. Whether we are idle at home or in the midst of some busy task, our minds are always active in a negative or a positive way and is a fertile resting place for a plethora of thoughts.

Negativity is developed in our thinking when we get influenced by negative news and views floating around generally in our immediate surrounding. News of disasters, health issues, the loss of a possession, nay even a piece of gossip conveyed over the phone could alter the mental status of an individual, albeit temporarily. Talking about gossip, one must remember that 'an idle mind is a devil's workshop'. Without any constructive thought or any positive activity occupying the mind of an individual, it becomes almost impossible for him to wean away from the debilitating effects of negative thoughts. The mind then gets cluttered with a whole lot of destructive thoughts, mostly from the past, which tend to lead the individual astray from any fruitful activity or enterprise. It is, therefore, not without reason that Wayne L. Misner, the noted Canadian writer has said, 'Keeping baggage from the past will leave no room for happiness in the future'. It is only with a conscious, deliberate attempt to stay clear of such unnecessary thoughts that an individual could emerge with a positive bent of mind.

Talking about positivity, when an individual discards depressing and infructuous thoughts, he or she would experience the flow of a lot of positivity into the space that would have fallen vacant in the mind. While working at creating a credit card brand for Bank of America, Dee Ward Hock helped invent the Visa Card and, in his words, 'Clean out a corner of your mind and creativity will instantly fill it'. Even Buddha had ordained that, 'We are shaped by our thoughts; we become what we think. When the mind is pure, joy follows like a shadow that never leaves'. The bottom line, therefore, is that stuffing our minds with decadent and immaterial thoughts will in no way lead us to happiness and peace of mind. This aspect has been exemplified by a popular song from the Bollywood movie *Kaajal* (1965), the lyrics of which were penned by the legendary poet, Sahir Ludhianvi. The first stanza of the song goes as under:

Mann hi devta, mann hi Ishwar, mann se bada na koi;
Mann ujiyara jab jab phayle, jag ujiyara hoi,
Is ujle darpan par prani,
Dhool na jamne payey.

A simple translation of this reads as follows: The mind is God, there is nothing more superior than the mind; whenever the radiance of the mind spreads around, the universe becomes radiant and in this radiant mirror, let no dust be allowed to gather. So beautifully said, the essence of the stanza reiterates that the hallowed mind is the abode of the Almighty and no dirt should be allowed to mar its radiance.

When the mind, therefore, is cleansed of its avoidable and retrogressive thoughts, it is calmed to become the ultimate weapon against all our battles. As a saying goes, 'Quiet the mind, and the soul will speak'. A calm mind then becomes a reservoir of energy which cannot be destroyed by frivolous banter. As the famous philosopher, Aristotle, enunciates, 'The energy of the mind is the essence of life'. It is, indeed, paramount that we adhere to this simple philosophy of keeping our minds light with positive thoughts and constantly refrain from loading it with sensational, depressing and self-defeating thoughts which could bring about the ruination of our thought-process, albeit the very essence of our being.

TWELVE

A FALL GUY CALLED FATE

The school ground was teeming with students as the practise for the school sports meet was underway. Vikas was attempting the high jump using the Fosbury Flop technique. His coach stood by and watched him run up and launch himself and then knock the bar down. He had already tried more than half-a-dozen times and each time he faulted owing to his heel or some part of his body nudging the bar and bringing it down. "Don't lose heart. Keep trying, you'll succeed," remarked his coach, Sunder, nonchalantly. His stoic calmness put Vikas at rest and inspired him to 'keep trying' till he succeeded.

Vikas could consider himself to be lucky, for not everyone gets the sort of encouragement, motivation and opportunity to keep on trying until success is achieved. Not every trial would lead to imminent success but a discipline of making an effort on a continuous basis, leads to a regimen of experiencing success as a matter of routine. It is said that success is not a destination but a journey. Even so, segments of this journey would offer opportunities for an individual to feel elated on achievement of a perceived elevation of activity. However, the journey itself is often mired in hindrances which sometimes are so convoluted that it is indeed quite an ordeal to weave one's way through the morass. Nevertheless, an individual needs to be steadfast to his goal and with perseverance make cognitive progress towards it. If a person's effort is spirited and dedicated, he would, in all probability, achieve success much sooner than he would have expected; however, if the effort is frivolous and half-hearted, it results in nothing but a drain of his energy.

At this juncture, more often than not, the individual is tempted to resign to his sloppy condition and blame his fate for everything that has gone amiss. Fate then becomes the fall guy upon which the ignominy of defeat or loss is heaped to provide temporary solace to the unsuccessful soul. How very strange and stupid of us to even assign fate with all the slips that may befall us! The failure of an effort to fructify into success lies in either it being insincere or plain ineffective. Deficiency in our effort cannot and must not be assigned to the hand of fate. 'Failure only happens when you lose your willpower to continue trying...If we let the obstacles get the best of us, then it was our choice to fail, not fate', says Lindsey Rietzsch, the famous singer and song-writer. How true that in the scheme of the cosmos, luck and fate do not have any part to play, except that it provides a temporary reprieve from our unfortunate delinquencies, deliberate or otherwise. We need to appreciate the fact that we are responsible for whatever is happening in our lives. By trying to relegate a distasteful turn of events to fate we are entering the realm of escapism, and that by no means is the signature of a courageous person.

Granted that a person has failed in his attempt to achieve whatever he wanted to. It is then that he needs to introspect and define where he had faulted in his attempt. If he steps back and takes his defeat positively, he, no doubt, may have lost his battle but would not forget the lesson emanating from the loss. And that is the greatest service that defeat does to an individual who refuses to be cowed down by the temporary decline in stature. For, 'failure does not define you. It's what you do *after you fail* that determines whether you are a leader or a waste of perfectly good air', says Sabaa Tahir, the distinguished best-selling American author. Nothing could be further from the truth. In a similar vein, Chris Bradford, the celebrated English author and martial artist, has commented, 'There is no failure, remember, except in no longer trying. It is courage to continue that counts'.

It is the inner strength of an individual which will accept the reality of failure as being a stepping stone to success, rather than finding refuge in fate. In the words of Eleanor Roosevelt, the former first lady of America and a political figure and diplomat in her own right, 'No man is defeated without until he has first been defeated within'.

In conclusion, therefore, we must accept that by assigning the reasons of failure to fate, one only exposes the frivolousness and weakness of character, as it is only a person with maturity, stature and willingness to look within, who can cast away thoughts of being a victim of fate.

THIRTEEN

The Perils of Overconfidence

Vaman was brimming with pride. He had been selected for a reality quiz show which was basically in the realm of general knowledge and offering substantial amounts of money at each stage of the game. He had been trying for years together, undaunted by failure at every attempt and now, finally, had passed the audition and was on his way to Mumbai to be a part of the recording of the programme.

At the recording, he was tantalized by the superb sets, lighting, etc. and, of course, the celebrated anchor. But he was confident – rather *over-confident.* And why shouldn't he be, he thought. After all he had topped in several quiz competitions from his school days and had even represented his country in international quiz meets.

The recording commenced and the questions began to flow with periodic frequency. His answers were quick and convincing. Even the anchor was bowled over by his vast knowledge and perspective and commended him after each correct answer. Vaman was afforded the privilege of using three lifelines if he was in doubt regarding an answer. Even after proceeding briskly to the first level of guaranteed prize money, he had not used a single lifeline and he wanted to use these later on in the game as the questions were tougher and the amount of money involved increased exponentially. He had set his sights on the apex question which would fetch him a tidy sum plus an expensive car as a bonus. As he advanced further in the game, he began to feel more confident and, in the process, more complacent; and that was his undoing. Three questions later and with all his lifelines intact, he ventured to answer the subsequent question without batting an eyelid, even though he wasn't entirely sure of the answer. The anchor, on his part, prior to putting forth the question, had advised him to use the lifelines that were still available; but Vaman was confident that he was pouting out the correct answer. He was too sure of himself. In a second, the scenario changed; Vaman had answered incorrectly and had to forfeit a lot of prize money he had already earned.

It is easy to appreciate what actually happened in Vaman's case. He was not only sure he could answer the question, but he was too sure that he could do so without any help or assistance. He had entered the phase of being over-confident and that proved to be a disaster for him. As Oscar Wilde rightly says, 'Confidence is good, but overconfidence always *sinks* the ship'. It's a very thin line between being confident and over-confident that Vaman had deliberately crossed which led to his sudden downfall.

The right amount of confidence is imperative in any constructive activity that we undertake, e.g. building a reputation over a period, building an edifice, building trust, etc. where the admixture of maturity and wisdom will guide an individual to achieve levels of success without having to stick his neck out in a brazen manner. The moment the self-imposed circle of activity is pursued with a sense of gay abandon, on account of the individual being over-confident with himself, all that he had gained assiduously and painstakingly over a length of time would come crashing down like a pack of cards.

If this be the case, one would wonder, what is it that induces a person to be over-confident. An analysis of cases, where people have lost out being successful at various stages of their lives, would reveal that pride, arrogance and greed are intertwined in a debilitating cocktail to mould an individual towards pushing further on his path with nil or incomplete knowledge of where is heading. This is the blinding stage of an individual's performance of an activity and is symptomatic of reckless often haughty behaviour patterns which evidently succumb to the ignominy of an obvious defeat. In the example that has been elucidated above, Vaman was so much consumed in assessing the proclivity of amassing as much prize money as possible, that he did not have the presence of mind to take one step at a time and cross the bridges as they come. How true was Harold Washington, the former mayor of Chicago, referring to predictions of results of the mayoral poll, when he stated, 'Let's not be overconfident, we still have to count the votes'.

Again, while confidence exuded by an individual ensures that he is humble though capable, overconfidence displays an erratic behaviour inspired by a convoluted mind. While confidence would imbue a feeling of 'I can do it', overconfidence oversteps this line and dictates that 'I *only* can do it'. It is essential to appreciate from this, that overconfidence, in most cases, is confidence plus ego. It is not for nothing that our forefathers had spelt out that pride goes before a fall; they had spoken from experience. It is well worth our while to ingrain this small lesson in our persona as we go along the journey called life.

FOURTEEN

THE MARK OF GREATNESS

Rakesh was not in the habit of committing anything during his utterances with his relatives but, being an affectionate and empathetic individual, was often prone to extending his help and doing favours for others in a quiet and unassuming way without a whimper. His concern for his relatives was salutary as was his willingness to ever stick his neck out for them. “They are after all part of my family in one way or the other. How can I ever forsake them in any hour of crisis?” he was wont to say, much to the admiration of his select audience. He was the epitome of care and concern for all those around him.

There are several people like Rakesh in our midst – people who prefer to help and care for others, especially relatives, in an unseen way. They are not in search of praise or laurels but find contentment in cushioning the ever-burgeoning problems that surface in the lives of others. This is not to say that they are blind to the problems within their own nuclear families. While they do attend to these with a ‘charity begins at home’ attitude, they, nevertheless, do not rest until they have probably done at least one good deed every day to someone in the family. They are the saviours, benefactors or what have you in the journey of life who are always available at somebody's beck and call, ready to deliver to their best possible extent. These are the men and women who take upon themselves the mantle of helping others become great.

True greatness does not lie in running the race of life with a singular mind, devoid of feelings and concern for others. That would be the ultimate in self-aggrandizement and selfishness as it would inculcate tendencies to be mercenary and ruthless. Instead, a truly great soul is one that would be sensitive to others in the race along with him, such that he would encourage the ascendancy to greatness of the other individual even at the cost of his own well-being. This would be the extreme sacrifice that would endear such an individual to others. In due course, he would often become the go-to person for everyone and one who seldom, if ever, comes under the spotlight. This is the individual who works behind the scenes for the betterment of others, like a good Samaritan or a bulwark never failing.

Bob Marley, the Jamaican singer and one of the pioneers of reggae had once said, 'The greatness of a man is not in how much wealth he acquires, but his integrity and his ability to *affect those around him positively'*. In a similar vein, Martin Luther King Jr. had this to say, 'Everyone has the power for greatness, not for fame, but greatness, because *greatness is determined by service'*. When we let go of our egos and engage in wilful and limitless service to all those who are primarily near and dear to us, we usher in an era of camaraderie and hope to all those who look up to us for help in some way or the other. How true this is when we can appreciate the fact that greatness is not about how you feel as a consequence of your positive actions but about what feelings of upliftment you have created in others.

Even Benjamin Disraeli, the former PM of UK, was emphatic when he declared at a convention, 'A great person is one who affects the mind of a generation'. It is imperative, therefore, in this context that greatness will transcend the environs of an individual or his team and spread its influence over a wide populace. Lives will be touched and destinies carved out for many who come within the ambit of such an influence.

Moreover, greatness of an individual is a measure of how he reaches out to the common man. Compassion for the less privileged and marginalized is in essence the sign of a great person. How often have we seen people around us who after having achieved a certain degree of success in their lives tend to forget the path by which they had come by. None could have described this scenario more graphically than Shakespeare in Julius Caesar when in Act II Scene I, Brutus says, '... The abuse of greatness is when it disjoins remorse from power... but 'tis a common proof, that lowliness is young ambition's ladder, whereas the climber upward turns his face; but when he once attains the upmost round, he then unto the ladder turns his back, looks in the clouds, scorning the base degrees by which he did ascend'. A person who succumbs to his ego will never experience the effect, if at all, that his actions have upon others. On the contrary, it would be a person's sign of greatness if, in spite of his achievements, he is firmly grounded and among the circle of people whose company he cherishes.

FIFTEEN

CATCHES WIN MATCHES BUT...

Prashant peered through the window of his study at the young lads playing cricket in the park abutting the service road adjacent to his house. Mahesh Shringarpure, his neighbour's son, was tossing the ball in his hands at the top of his bowling run-up, while simultaneously issuing some instructions to the deep fielders with some time-tested gestures. Then, in a jiffy he had delivered, what seemed to Prashant, as being a 'good length' ball. The batter had a swipe, then there was an appeal and a round of clapping – the batter had been caught by the fielder at 'mid-wicket', obviously as a result of a mis-timed shot. Prashant, now forty-five and having retired from first class cricket, looked on as *all* the balance ten players in the fielding side, apart from the bowler, ran up to the latter for giving him a 'well-deserved' pat and hug for his 'tremendous' achievement. The bowler was on the moon. The fielder who had taken the catch, meanwhile, looked around to see if he was getting any kudos and, probably to satiate his expectation, a couple of players on their way to congratulate the bowler, patted him as if to dole him out a consolation prize, while he converged towards the centre of the pitch to be with the rest of his team who were waiting for the next batter to come in from the pavilion.

For a moment, an instance where he had taken a fairly difficult catch near the boundary during one of the matches in his career, flashed before Prashant. He'd been a regular fielder at 'long-off' and a highly regarded one at that, for hardly had a probable catch that came his way ever been dropped. But he recollected the write-up by the correspondent of *Morning News* on that occasion, where the latter had lauded the bowler in the particular situation as being the 'demolition man'. Apart from a mere mention of him having taken a catch, there was no reference to Prashant in the write-up. He had felt side-lined in the description of the glory that followed with the fall of the wicket. But that instance was fairly early in his career, and he had since that time learned his paces the hard way – play your game and let the credit find its own resting place. For this was the philosophy that Prashant Solkar always carried uppermost in his mind as he sailed through his commendable career with excellence and elan.

Many of us in our lives and careers have been in situations often faced by Prashant. We may have done a good job, nay an excellent one, in our working careers but ultimately the credit for it would have gone to another individual higher up in the corporate hierarchy. Now, if the latter had been humble to admit that he would not have achieved what he did without the support and help from his subordinates, probably the credit would have been spread over a wider canvas of individuals, at least in the short run; else, the effort of his subordinates would have been relegated to the lesser-known facts of corporate history, probably with a mention by way of a post-script.

Well, that is the hard fact that one learns in the job, profession or calling that one engages in to earn his livelihood, namely that it does not matter who gets the credit for a job well done, rather what matters is that one plays the game or his part to the best of his ability. Even in the particular case of him taking a spectacular catch to dismiss the batter, Prashant recollected that the credit given to the bowler was short-lived, for the ultimate credit went to the captain for winning the match.

This brings me to the all-important fact that credit for achieving a superb result cannot be savoured by all who are instrumental in making it possible. Rather, it is that elusive tiara that finds its way to adorn the head of only one individual who is the captain of the ship. Take the case of a movie; when it becomes a hit at the box-office, it's the director who gets the credit and in fact hogs the limelight. Of course, the performances of the lead actors would be commented upon and commended in appropriate forums, but the one who stands out from the crowd would be the director. Or, let us consider the role of a conductor in an orchestra. Every musician plays his part in the overall music score, but the man waving the baton ultimately is the focus of the applause that follows a performance, as he bows low before an august audience. Similarly, there can be numerous examples where credit finally rests with one individual who is the leader of the team.

Prashant placed the cup of tea back on the saucer as he reverted to the present moment. Yes, indeed, in all his career in first class cricket, he had excelled in the areas of batting and fielding and had played the game as he best thought fit in the circumstances coupled with the advice received from his captain and coach. He had not dwelt on the prospect of receiving applause and credit for his actions as he felt that would have clouded his performance. Bereft of these thoughts, he had only one aim in his mind and that was to see how his performance would enhance the overall performance of his team. He had realized very early on in his career that his role was, as everybody else's, contributory to the team effort and that he had to play his part in the best possible way as per the circumstances, for his team and his nation and not for his own self.

Prashant arranged the drapes back in place and as he moved away from the window, his eyes fell on a poster which was within a frame and hanging from the wall. On it was written a message from the Bhagavad Gita, loud and clear: *The meaning of Karma is in the intention. The intention behind the action is what matters. Those who are motivated only by the fruits of action are miserable, for they are constantly anxious about the results of what they do.* 'How true,' thought Prashant, as he smiled inwardly and proceeded towards the dining room where lunch was being laid out by his wife.

SIXTEEN

ADDING COLOUR TO LIFE

Have we ever wondered how colourful is the world around us? We may have done so whenever we had the time and inclination for it. The colours of nature like the lush green trees and multihued flora, the hills and mountains with their peaks rising up to skim the skies causing tufts of grey and white clouds to agglomerate around them are awesome in every detail. Or take the example of vast landscapes bathed in green with abutting roadsides lined with bushes, shrubs and trees of various colours which are imposing as we drive down the countryside, or the vastness of a desert with its shifting sand dunes are other manifestations of the colourful beauty of nature which is endless and bountiful and needs to be observed to be appreciated.

In a similar vein man-made beauty in this world lends colour to our daily lives. It could be the grandiosity of a large shopping mall affording pleasure and convenience to shop or the extravagance of a children's fun park with its variety of brightly coloured games equipment and food stalls. Whatever it is, colours definitely play a major part in moulding our lives, our temperament and thought processes. Without colour around us, life would have been prosaic and loaded with ennui.

Human beings, too, are colourful with each in his or her own way. Some may choose to be colourful externally by dressing up tastefully in coloured fabrics which blend with each other, coupled with a dose of grooming and appropriate footwear. This is generally the trend that one sees nowadays in the generation that is still coming of age and searching for a stable grounding in life. Many among them, however, also have the colourfulness that is derived from their august upbringing, education, friends' circle and above all their inter-personal skills. This colour is internal but is manifest in everything that the individual does or says. It is the exuberance of the spirit within, that casts its colourful rays in several wonderful ways with each passing day.

It is an excellent trait to be intrinsically colourful in life, for that will carry the individual through all the peaks and troughs in the trials and tribulations of life. Such an individual will know the benefits of being calm in crisis, patient and tolerant in times of stress, humorous and joyful in the company of people and confident and firm while having to take a decision. They will exude the characteristics of a mature individual with a foresight seldom seen. In the words of Amy Leigh Mercree, author with a large following on social media, '*Be uniquely you. Stand out. Shine. Be colourful*'. In an age where there is a down-turn in the economy everywhere, causing loss of jobs and opportunities, it becomes even more important to stay grounded and be ourselves. It is possible that somebody may not like you – but that doesn't matter. You need to hold on to your horses, and not be beguiled, for almost everyone who may not be in sync with you, could actually be struggling to like themselves.

A colourful personality will find a way to look at each situation in his life with the colour that he feels suits best. For example, in a situation of crisis, where everyone around may see red, the colourful person who is wise, will stay focused on the solution to the crisis and see a colour, probably green, because he knows that the solution to the problem lies within the problem itself. As John Homer Mills, the writer of eminence who has been credited with publishing the first complete treatise on all branches of agriculture, says, '*Circumstances and situations do colour life, but you have been given the mind to choose what the colour shall be*'.

But, by far, the greatest service that a colourful person could provide to the people around him is to cast aside any semblance of ego or arrogance and meld in the colours of the social fabric around him by adding colour to the lives of others. In doing so, he would be not only be displaying his humility and concern for others but also arranging a platform to provide a hallmark for appropriate advice and line of action. The late Maya Angelou, noted author, poet and civil rights activist, had once stated, '*Try to be a rainbow in someone's cloud*'. In a similar vein, Ms. Mercree had this to say, '*The world needs your prismatic soul*'. By lending colour to the lives of others, you are at once elevated in their eyes and a benefactor of their blessings. Always available for spreading colour or lighting a candle in someone's life, a colourful personality understands that blowing out somebody else's candle, would not make his shine better or brighter.

There can be probably no greater canvas than life itself. Human beings would do well to splash this canvas with as many hues as possible for the betterment of mankind.

SEVENTEEN

POSITIVE VIBES FROM 'NO'

"No, I would not be able to come for your 'housewarming' ceremony next week," said Lokesh, addressing his friend, Raghav. The latter was crestfallen. He had looked forward to seeing his buddy come over to see his new house which he had built with so much care and dedication.

"When will you be able to make it to my home?" persisted Raghav.

"I do not know. The exigencies in my work, at the moment, will not permit me any spare time."

The tone of negativity, though not deliberate, was enough to put off Raghav for the time being at least.

Far away, in another city, a rebellious teenager was throwing tantrums at his father, "No, I do not wish to continue my studies."

The devastated father, who had nurtured ambitions of his son becoming an engineer, pleaded with his son to reconsider his decision, but to no avail.

In both the above scenarios, one can appreciate the negativity that can percolate quickly with the use of the word, 'no'. It is like the dead-end of any communication between two or more individuals that provides no recourse for any further discussion. It is for this reason, therefore, that the word 'no' has developed to be the curt and terse epitome of a deadlock in communication or a precursor for inaction.

But there's a sunny side also to the word 'no', which when used deftly, can transcend all barriers of communication and action with its munificent positivity and forthright transparency. I am referring to the use of the word, as in the following thought-process of a strong-willed individual who has failed in his first attempt to swim across a lake. He would probably be telling himself, 'No, I cannot allow this to happen to me. I must be able to get across the lake, else I would not be able to perform in the upcoming competition'. Or let us consider the example of a student who has failed in his exam. He must be able to gather himself to say, "No, I can't allow this failure to put me down. I have probably not given my best this time and need to introspect and improve my performance. I will try again and emerge with flying colours." Only then there is hope for him to succeed in his very next attempt.

The word, 'no', when used in the two instances in the preceding paragraph, conveys a tumultuous avalanche of emotions relating to grit, will-power and a 'I can' attitude to perform. When used in this way, the word is the very antithesis of all that it is otherwise perceived to be. It then has the power of refuting failure, inaction and a block in communication with a surge of energy that kindles the thought that whatever negativity has transpired is only transitory and can be remedied with a will to perform and succeed. So, the next time you face a difficult situation in life, don't hesitate to cobble up your energies into one solid force and say to yourself, "No, I'm not going to take this lying down, because I can do better to surmount this obstacle." That is the spirit of positivity that 'no' projects when used with a 'never say die' attitude. It helps one to rediscover, recharge, react and reinvent whatever one may have been unsuccessful in one's initial attempt; and that is an opportunity being fuelled with a great degree of optimism.

There is yet another aspect of 'no' which, besides stirring one to action, embodies the strength to refute someone from taking you for granted. An individual may experience at some point in life that people, who may be near and dear, expect him to perform a task as a matter of rote even though it may not be in his usual scheme of things. Such incidents where a person is bypassed in even taking his consent must be avoided by the individual with a firm 'no'. It is better to say 'no' out of strength than to say 'yes' with a weak bent of mind. Dodinsky, a NY Times best-selling author and emerging leader in positive thinking, says in a similar vein, '*To be happy is to wisely use the power of saying No to some people. Don't be afraid to disappoint people who only conveniently remember you when they want something from you*'.

The word, 'no', therefore, when used in the right context symbolizes a powerful and positive communication tool not only for oneself but also for all those to whom a message is sought to be delivered.

EIGHTEEN

A JOURNEY CALLED SUCCESS

It was a moment of exultation. A courier had just delivered a parcel to Prasad and as the latter retrieved a shining trophy from its confines, his mother, seeing his joyous countenance, remarked in no uncertain terms, "Now, that's what is called success." Prasad was speechless as the full facade of the trophy radiated on his face in the sharp rays of the mid-morning sun. His mother gave him a hug even as the thought of having won a laurel for his efforts was still sinking into him. He was an amateur singer who would participate in several competitions and reality shows. It was in one of these contests that he had been declared the winner although unfortunately he could not make it to the grand award function on account of his indisposition.

As his mother proceeded towards the kitchen to cook up his favourite *biryani*, Prasad contemplated on what his mother had said. Was this achievement akin to success? Or was it a pleasant occurrence on the road to success? He could not rationalize at that moment, as the euphoria of having won a trophy had still not died down.

Most of us would have passed through at some stage in our lives the joyful moment that Prasad had encountered. Yet how many of us would have looked upon such an authentication of our talent as just a feather in the cap? Some of us, being the pompous lot, would have strutted around like peacocks as if they had reached the zenith of their efforts, while the humbler lot would have decided to take the accolade in their stride such that it did not influence their bigger picture of being on the continuous path towards excellence.

That brings me to the core issue of the concept of success. There are so many opinions and connotations adorning this idea, that often an achiever may be swayed by a thought that rushes to his mind on an impulse. According to me, complete success is illusory for the simple reason that nobody has all the time to achieve all the things he had wanted to, in the manner that he would have desired and acknowledged by one and all. What anybody does is surmount obstacles in his path that paves the way for him to experience a recognition for his efforts. In the process, he enjoys the luxury of occasional bouts of satisfaction as he traverses along the road towards success. This, indeed, is the vision of success where it is viewed not as a destination but as a journey. An analogy for success, therefore, would be conceiving it as a highway where one is travelling with a definite purpose. During this journey, one takes time off to rest at lay-bys and refreshes and rejuvenates oneself before continuing on the journey. Along the highway, milestones pass by which could be referred to as fleeting reassurances that one is proceeding in the right direction. This is similar to an occasional sense of achievement which results in temporary spells of joy.

Another point to be noted is that the intermittent occasions for rejoicing on the journey towards success are made possible only with a discipline of sustained efforts combined with focus, dedication and perseverance on the part of an individual. This has to necessarily be complemented by divine blessings. Only then would there be a sense of achievement on the part of the individual. The good wishes from well-wishers are channelized through the blessings from the Almighty and provide a spur for achieving greater laurels in future.

The road towards success is smooth when an individual undertakes to do what brings him the utmost happiness. As Albert Schweitzer rightly opines, 'Success is not the key to happiness. Happiness is the key to success. If you love what you are doing, you will be successful'. Helen Keller underscores this fact when she says, 'Your success and happiness lie in you'.

On the flip side, even when an individual fails several times in attempts to achieve a predetermined goal, he should not be depressed nor lose hope of ever being capable of achievement; for in those failed attempts, he should realize that he has discovered so many ways of doing things in an erroneous way. If he is able to appreciate this, then he would be wiser when he makes a fresh attempt to reach his objective. This aspect is vividly expounded by the Dalai Lama when he says, 'When you lose, don't lose the lesson'. It is, therefore, paramount to note that by giving up or accepting failure, we expose our weakness and the sure way to have a crowning glory for all our efforts is to try for just one more time.

The mind is a great warehouse of visualization where the fertile imagination of an individual who delves into his passion is rewarded with a fruitful culmination of his sustained efforts. A mind prodded on by inquiry will find new ways and newer ventures to whet its appetite for advancing in the journey towards success. There are, indeed, many paths we can take. We can choose to explore life with a spirit of adventure, or we can stay within a closed circle of comfort. It's not the place we live in, but our frame of mind that determines how far we go on our journey.

NINETEEN

PRESERVING ONE'S IDENTITY

I remember one of my classmates, Milind, in college who was very enamoured by the personality of Rajesh Khanna. He used to dress, maintain his hairstyle and even try to speak and emote like the legendary actor. No doubt Rajesh Khanna was a superstar and had a huge fan following and held sway over the Bollywood silver screen for several years before other actors took over from him. His films were all hit at the box office and the songs picturized on him and sung by another great artiste, Kishor Kumar, were on everybody's lips. But Milind was an exception. He used to be day-dreaming about the role of the actor in some recent movie that he had seen and even impress his circle of friends by pouting out some dialogue of the great actor which he had probably perfected after several rehearsals in front of the mirror. In a manner of speaking, he was consumed by the larger-than-life persona of Rajesh Khanna.

The case of Milind is not unique in our society. If we look around in our neighbourhood or in our work place, we may spot at least one individual, man or woman, who is living his or her life in the shadow of some celebrity who has influenced the mind of the individual to such an extent that his or her very own identity has been compromised, and the latter would have become almost an alter ego of the celebrity. And if the individual has some resemblance to such a personality which has been acknowledged in society, the craze to exude the mannerisms and mimic the celebrity becomes even more compelling.

It is not wrong for a person to be conscious of the fact that he resembles a celebrity. It is also not unnatural for him to probably project his appearance like the celebrity. After all, he is human. But that is about how far the matter should go. Any further inroads made to try and copy or imitate the celebrity would probably enthrall those around him, but his own identity would slowly but surely be on the path of erosion. The Almighty has made every individual unique with a specific set of skills. It is for the person to try and unravel this mystery during his lifetime. By trying to mimic another individual, except by way of a professional exercise, he not only goes against the laws of nature but also stunts his own skill set which could otherwise bring him laurels if developed in the course of his life. Even the common understanding, which has been proven scientifically, that for every individual there are six others, apart from twins, somewhere on the planet who resemble him, also would be people who, in all probability, are mentally poles apart.

So, this brings us to the all-important function of preserving one's own identity. While it may be sensible to have a good role model in life, every person should live his life as naturally as possible. Bereft of any fixations and complexes, a person will be able to carve out his own identity which would be appreciated by everyone with whom he interacts from time to time. Rather than towing the mannerisms, behaviour and lifestyle of another, a person would probably be able to influence many others by his unique personality. As Peter Frampton, the well-known English guitarist, singer and songwriter, opines, 'Your own material is your identity, and I think that's what you need to stick to'. How true, therefore, that one should have confidence in one's own abilities for that is what will help him carve out his own identity. Ralph Waldo Emerson espouses the concept in a similar vein when he says, 'To be yourself in a world that is constantly trying to make you something else is the greatest accomplishment'.

Indeed, to develop and retain one's own identity one needs to be resourceful and resolute and should reinvigorate and reinvent. In a dynamic world, it remains a challenge for anyone to preserve one's own identity and individualism. 'If you really have your own identity', advises Helmut Lang, the famous fashion designer, 'you'll keep on doing what you think is really right for you and you'll also understand the next step you want to take'. Therefore, irrespective of the family that we are born into, we need to become ourselves by choosing and creating our paths in the manner that best projects our separate identities. Only then will we be in a position to add value to our lives and to the lives of those around us.

TWENTY

STICKING ONE'S NECK OUT

It was a bright and sunny day, the ideal setting for a cricket match, with a waft of gentle breeze blowing over the lush green ground, as Naresh ran in from the pavilion end to bowl the next delivery to Vijay. A good length ball it was, rising gradually outside the off stump, which could have been conveniently avoided by Vijay. However, the lad hung his bat out just as the ball whizzed past him, giving rise to the dreaded snick and almost simultaneous appeal by the wicketkeeper which confirmed the worst to the rapt spectators who had crowded around the boundary line. The umpire's forefinger went up immediately even as Vijay had proceeded to walk towards the pavilion. He had lost his wicket, caught behind the stumps, just as he was crawling in the nervous nineties.

Vijay's predicament is akin to a common problem which many of us face in our lives. It's called 'hanging your bat out' and every time this happens, it is both unnecessary and risky. It gets one involved in a situation which could have been best avoided and then the aftermath of it all is that one is embarrassed and more often than not on the brink of failure.

This phenomenon is also loosely known as 'sticking one's neck out'. However, in a particular aspect of this case, a person takes the initiative to involve himself in an activity which results in a benefit to another. There are many examples of this. One of these could be that an individual X recommends another person Y, generally someone close to him, for a job to a third person Z. Now, Z would employ Y on the basis of the trust and relationship that he would be having with X. After Y has taken up the employment with Z, X would presume that everything is hunky dory and he has done something to accentuate his good karma. He is not wrong because he has been instrumental in providing a livelihood to Y, where the latter probably had none. But things may not turn out to be just the way that X thought it would be. Y, after commencing work in his new employment, could have felt that the job was not to his liking or that he is being paid less than he had expected. Sooner than later, therefore, he would construct imaginary huge walls or mountains before him which delude him to feel that the job is not meant for him and that he should quit at the earliest. Driven by this consummate feeling, he leaves the employment, probably even without informing X, who had recommended him for the job. Later on, when X is aware of what has transpired, he is embarrassed and unable to face Z, at least in the short run. Z, on his part, would be expecting a gracious apology from X on behalf of Y, which probably would not be forthcoming, as he may yet not be aware of Y's exit from the employment. This causes unnecessary misunderstanding between X and Z, all because of Y. In hindsight, X would be constrained to ponder that, had he not taken the initiative to recommend

Y for a job, he would still be on a strong wicket as regards his relationship with Z. But then, unfortunately, too much water would have flowed under the bridge and it would probably take a herculean effort on the part of X to set things right.

However, the flip side and bright spot in this is that if X were to have tremendous confidence in Y and the latter were to have unwavering loyalty for X, then it would be feasible for X to stick his neck out for Y and yet get the praise from Z, for having recommended a worthy person to work in his employ. So, the lesson one needs to learn is that sticking one's neck out for another is only advisable if there is an abiding relationship of trust and confidence between the two.

The other aspect is that it is often advantageous and advisable to stick one's neck out for oneself. This means that a person who takes initiative and risks for his own advancement may, albeit, face hurdles but these should be regarded as temporary aberrations and he would surely see light at the end of the tunnel in the long run. As the famous adage, 'Nothing risked, nothing gained' is so ingrained in everybody's psyche, it would make sense to implement this dictum whenever the opportunity arises. A turtle, for example, does not move forward if it does not stick its neck out. So also, the giraffe does not get to eat the fresh green leaves high up on an acacia tree if it were not to stretch and stick its neck out to the maximum. So it is, in every one's life – if, instead of hiding in a shell, we measure up to confront the challenges that stare at us in our face on a daily basis we'll be able to move on in life, unnerved by the risks or difficulties involved along the way.

TWENTY-ONE

CONSISTENCY IN ACTION

Ganesh was a bright student in an English-medium public school and now in standard VIII, had passed with flying colours. The time had come for him to choose the appropriate stream of study as per his aptitude. Would it be science, commerce or humanities? His parents advised him to take up science since he was good in Maths and Physics. And so, it turned out that he joined the science stream and did well for himself the next year, too. Going by his marks in all the preceding years, Ganesh had stood out academically as being a model student and was the cynosure of his teachers' eyes who saw in him, a scholar in the making. But fate had other plans for him and, in the vulnerable age that he was, Ganesh fell into bad company and soon became the bane for his parents and his teachers in school. In the ensuing board exams, Ganesh fared badly and even failed in one subject. His parents and teachers were aghast, but the damage was done.

What do we get to learn from the sad chapter in Ganesh's life? Yes, it is about taking control of one's life and not letting it dither even for a moment. Focus on a perceived goal is the principal requirement coupled with dedication towards its achievement. Along the way, the individual should have the presence of mind and be alert to distractions and disruptions that may wean him away from his objective. Only then, would he be able to perform consistently. Consistency, therefore, is a precursor of excellence which again leads one towards perfection.

However, consistency in action by itself is not important. The intent of doing an action in a repetitive style and pattern is as important as the action itself, as the nature of the final result would be judged on the basis of the goodness it radiates. The quality of consistency in one's life comes through sheer habit of performing actions in a particular way. For example, an individual who is involved in smuggling goods systematically across the border of his country, would no doubt be consistent in ensuring that he is able to deliver with repetitive success and still not be caught in the process. However, his consistency in his underhand dealings would probably earn him respect in the underworld, but his actions, being intrinsically illegal and unethical, would invite trouble not only for him but for everyone who depends on him for their livelihood. On the contrary, a person who is consistent in bringing laurels to his country in sports would be lauded for his sustained efforts in surpassing the limits of excellence, every time he performs. Consistency of action, therefore, implies an inherent sense of integrity and honesty to be woven into its fabric.

Consistency in a noble action is what enables an individual to proceed on the path of progress. Whenever a person executes a genuine action, he would experience a momentary feeling of success. This is natural, but if were not to linger on the temporary exultation and instead create a regimen for himself to perform the action with consistency and sustained success, he would lead himself towards progress. This is what isolates this individual from the rest of the crowd who may perform actions which do not even skim the bar of success.

To be consistent, one needs to possess an underlying mindset which is focused on the task at hand. One may be having all the resources at his command such as intellect, dedication, tenacity, etc., but if the basic element of concentration or focus is not present, the resources would be frittered away in due course. It is focus which is the driving force for enabling a task, consistently executed, to be successful and then with such repeated performances, the individual paves his path towards progress. It is often said that a tenacious person will get what he is aiming at but it is only a consistently focused individual who will get to keep it.

A major ingredient in consistency is believing in oneself. Self-confidence is an accepted norm for achieving consistency in action. One may try to do repetitive actions without any zeal or passion and will end up without a clue as to where is headed. It is, therefore, necessary to be convinced of your goal and inculcate the confidence to achieve it by dedicated execution.

It's not what we achieve once in a while like flashes in the pan that will awe us and those around us; it is what we are able to effect consistently that will finally call the shots. Everything that is perceived to have value in life is gained through consistency. All that people aspire like fitness, health, success and wealth, as well as friendships and relationships are nothing but a result of consistent action. If only everyone understood the importance of being consistent, the world would be a better place to live and enjoy the benefits that accrue.

TWENTY-TWO

A PROMISE MADE...

Not much in use today, promissory notes were very much in vogue in mercantile trade in decades gone by. 'I promise to pay...' was how the draft of the document would begin, which entailed the promise of one individual to another in respect of the payment of a certain sum of money on a particular date for goods or services received. The document embellished an irrevocable intent of the debtor to pay his creditor on the due date. Thus, it measured up to the much-misunderstood quote, 'A promise made is a debt unpaid'.

But is it that in every case a promise needs to be in writing, or are even verbal commitments and assurances a part of the wide canvas of promises, however casually these may have been pouted? The answer is 'Yes', for in the normal way of life in a society, a 'gentleman's word' is to be respected as being one which assures the execution of a certain deed in a specified timeframe.

Why then do I term the quote as having been 'misunderstood'? Because, not everyone appreciates the significance or the seriousness in which a commitment or promise is given by one person to another. More often than not, in everyday interactions between people, promises are made not with the specific intent to ensure its execution or compliance, but rather to ward off the disquiet generated by an aggravated argument or to part company from a person, albeit temporarily, who is being over-insistent on getting a commitment for his proposal. In both these cases, like in many other instances, a promise is registered by word of mouth but never honoured, because *ab initio*, it was not intended to be.

So, how does this affect the relationships between people? First of all, a person who indulges in making 'false promises' is soon ostracized in society as being one who has no integrity and people would always subsequently, therefore, take his utterances with a pinch of salt. Such people make a mockery of the genuineness of relationships built arduously over years of trust. They do not realize that 'promise' is a big word, which either makes something or breaks everything.

On the contrary, a person who honours his word, however casually made, lives in the memory of people as a 'man of his word'. Such an individual generates an aura around him and everyone respects him wherever he goes, for the story of his steadfastness to his word would have spread far and wide. Such people are few and far between, for they exude a genuine concern for others in their interactions with them. They may not be flashy and flamboyant in their utterances so as to make a show of their intentions, but they are the silent operators who have a steely resolve within, to execute what they have perceived to be a worthy action which may extend a benefit to others. They are often also dubbed, 'men of action', as they are wont to do what they have committed. Such people are welcome everywhere and are approached by others with a sense of confidence and trust in their interpersonal dealings.

People who make promises and keep them are winners in every sense of the term. These are erudite individuals who leave a trail of reliability and trust in their wake, wherever they go. They do not make promises which they feel they cannot keep but are honest and transparent enough to admit their inability to do a particular action when the execution and ramifications of it are being discussed. As Socrates has rightly said, 'A promise should be given with caution and kept with care'. Anthony Hitt, the well-known author, opines in a similar vein, 'Keep every promise you make and only make promises you can keep'. Aristotle is more emphatic when he says, 'A promise made must be a promise kept'. Yet others who make promises that they can often break are termed as losers for they do so, more often than not, to get the sadistic pleasure of breaking them. These are not individuals who are serious of cementing relationships but are flippant in their interactions with others. They are not concerned by the fact that breaking a promise is a bad thing even though that promise will ultimately break them.

For those of us who wish to keep up to our promises, it would be advisable to record these somewhere, maybe in a diary, so that we neither forget to act on those promises, nor the timeframe for doing so, in case there is one. And for the very meticulous amongst us, where keeping up to one's word is a way of life, indulging in the pleasures and happiness of the moment would hardly be of any consequence, for they are the ones who follow Robert Frost in his timeless verse,

The woods are lovely, dark and deep,

But I have promises to keep.
And miles to go before I sleep,
And miles to go before I sleep.

TWENTY-THREE

THE REALM OF TIME

It is the greatest resource in our lives, yet the most unpredictable. Always in continuous motion, it treats kings and commoners alike. It waits for none nor is it at anyone's beck and call. It calls the shots whenever a decision has to be taken. From the creation of the universe till the present moment, it has been man's constant companion, always available and accessible to provide him the duration to carry out his tasks. Never imposing itself on anyone, it has been the silent comrade-in-arms for being utilized for something fruitful. An individual goes about doing his duties, often oblivious of the fact that it is the most valuable resource in his life that is allowing him to complete his tasks. It infuses the realization in an individual to wake up each morning as it does to remind him to hit the sack for a good night's sleep, all the while goading him to walk that extra mile to achieve more, each day. I am referring to Time, which has been, is, and always will be the countervailing factor in everyone's lives.

Even though Time is a resource that is constantly being exhausted, whether it is utilized effectively or not, it does not preclude a person from achieving a certain goal at a later date. It offers multiple opportunities to man to reflect on what he has done, or could have done and correct himself, should the need arise, so that he has an enduring feeling of having completed his objectives in the manner that he had wished to. In so doing, therefore, an individual would feel elated at having achieved a milestone in his life, a feeling of *déjà vu* for being given opportunity to revisit his life's ambitions and to, therefore, embark on a journey of course correction, if required.

The famous adage, 'Time and tide wait for no man', is at once a call to duty as it is ominous. The essence of Time reflects the urgency to be on one's toes, lest the opportunity to exploit the moment is lost forever. For the achievement-oriented person, it is the Damocles sword over his head that constantly reminds him to put in more effort every minute of his life, so as to enjoy the comforts of life even though life itself, is fraught with worries, turbulence, violence and ultimate death. On the flip side, if the individual is callous, slovenly and a total wastrel, he will pay the penalty for his indolence in the twilight years of his life. As a verse in the famous lyrics by Shailendra for a song in the 1966 Bollywood movie, *Teesri Kasam*, brazenly analyses as follows,

Ladakpan khel mein khoya,
Jawaani neend bhar soya,
Bhudhaapaa dekh kar royaa,
Bhudhaapaa dekh kar royaa,
Wahi kissaa puraanaa hai

Simply said, it forbodes the warning that, should an individual waste his time in playing excessivelyin childhood or sleeping all the time in his youth, he would cry on seeing the onset of old age, a parable oft repeated, all to no avail. Time, which has gone by therefore, is much like the flow of water of a river which when having flowed into the sea, will never ever return to its original source of flow.

Time is also the all-pervasive witness of the goings-on in the world. An individual's career highs and lows, the growth of nations, the inconstancies of bourses, the vagaries of the oceans are all susceptible to the scrutiny of Time. That is why it is prudent for mankind to be 'afraid' of Time, for its trail can always change for better or for worse. This aspect has been aptly penned by Sahir Ludhianvi in the lyrics of the title song in the 1965 Bollywood movie, *Waqt,* a verse of which goes as under,

Aadmi ko chahiye, waqt se dar kar rahe,
Kaun jaane kis ghadi, waqt ka badle mizaaj,
Waqt ka badle mizaaj.

A simple translation of the above would be that 'human beings should be scared of Time for who knows when its mood would change'. This intrinsically refers to the demeanour of the individual. If he is humble, with a head over his shoulders, he would continue to flourish in his chosen vocation or field of activity; else, if he is the proud peacock brandishing his plumes unabashedly, he is sure to have a fall, sooner than later, for that is the way of the world. It is this unpredictable aspect of Time that requires a sensible individual to be always alert to not fall prey to the pitfalls occasioned by pride and ego.

Time is also the great healer. Tragedy brings concomitant grief in its wake but even here, it is Time, with its passing, which gradually causes the sorrow to wane before life again begins to move on as before.

Nothing, therefore, is permanent in the realm of Time. A child could be born in the same instant that another life is snuffed out. Whatever may happen, the wristwatch, the wall clock, the hourglass or the sundial would always be there to record the changes taking place in the diurnal course of our planet.

TWENTY-FOUR

Fly like a Balloon

Bhaskar gazed at the colourful pink and blue hues of the sky with tinges of orange interspersed alongside tufts of clouds as he stood in the balcony of his apartment with his five-year-old son, Ajay. The lad clutched his father's palm tightly as fear overtook the boy when he bent over to look at the road below. Suddenly, Bhaskar spotted a cluster of brightly-coloured balloons in the distance, steadily gaining height and he trained his eyes to look at the spectacle now flying high over the skyscrapers. Ajay looked up at his father and then in the direction where his dad seemed to be interested. Spotting the balloons he queried, "Daddy, why can't we fly like those balloons that we see yonder?"

His dad looked at him and smiled. "Because we are humans and human beings have not been created to fly," he explained with a nod of his head. But, no sooner than he had uttered those words, his forehead betrayed a frown and he gave a longing look at the receding sight of the balloons as they were swallowed by the clouds and soon disappeared from sight. "Even so, my son, the balloons have a greater tale to narrate to humans, than may be perceived. Come, let's go into the drawing room and I shall explain to you the lesson that we humans can learn from the flying balloons." So saying, Bhaskar led Ajay away from the balcony and seated the boy beside him on a sofa.

"A balloon flies because it is filled with a certain gas which provides it the lift," began Bhaskar. Ajay nodded in comprehension. "Human beings are made up of bones and flesh, the weight of which cause them to be grounded," explained Bhaskar. The twinkle in Ajay's eyes seemed to align with his father's reasoning. "However," continued Bhaskar, "human beings can fly if they wish to." Bhaskar paused in his discourse to see the reaction from his son. Ajay gave him a bewildered look that conveyed the message, 'how is that possible'?

Taking the cue, Bhaskar said, "I'll explain." Then he looked at his son squarely and stated, "human beings can fly if they discard the things that weigh them down."

"What are those things, daddy?"

"Pride, worries, hate, jealousy, etc., my child. These things are totally unnecessary in anybody's life and weigh down the mind of a person."

A semblance of realization seemed to dawn on Ajay's mind as his thoughts were distracted by an announcement by his mother from the kitchen that snacks had been laid out on the dining table.

The analogy of the flying balloons is extremely important in our daily lives. In the rat race that we see around us, there are umpteen opportunities to fall prey to our egos and be misled by false premises. These, in turn, give rise to wasteful tendencies that are a big draw on our precious energy. For example, we see that our neighbour has bought a new car and jealousy creeps into our mind.

Similarly, if a person has been sidelined by his boss in the office, he may nurture a grudge against him, which in time ripens to a full-fledged demeanour of hate towards his boss. A mother's genuine worries that accumulate with time with regard to her son's condition at work, in a distant land, tend to produce a drag on her happiness in her daily life. All these are simple but plausible examples how the human mind is weighed down by extraneous factors. These are akin to extra baggage that we tend to carry with us in our travels.

We need to be humble about instances which bring in appreciation from people around us, as these could easily cause us to succumb to pride and swollen-headedness. Our reaction, in all such cases, should be to graciously accept the adulations that are forthcoming but not get affected adversely by the tide of appreciation. Instead, the words of praise should help to bolster our self-confidence, not self-conceit. In like manner, for matters beyond our control, we must take a deliberate stance of detached attachment. In this way, instances which crop up time and again and seem to prick our base senses should be kept at bay and never encouraged to flourish.

A classic example that we can fall back upon which describes what pride can do, is illustrated in the play, *Julius Caesar*, by William Shakespeare. In it, Caesar is brutally assassinated by the Roman senators only because of his pride and all-consuming ambition to become the emperor of Rome. An instance of Caesar exuding his brazen pride is clear in the following lines, when he is petitioned by Metellus Cimber, a Roman, to show mercy to his brother and recall him from his banishment from Rome:

"I could be well moved, if I were as you;
If I could pray to move, prayers would move me:

But I am constant as the northern star, of whose true-fix'd and resting quality

There is no fellow in the firmament.
The skies are painted with unnumber'd sparks;
They are all fire and everyone doth shine;
But there's but one in all doth hold his place;
So in the world; 'tis furnish'd well with men,
An men are flesh and blood, and apprehensive;
Yet in the number I do know but one
That unassailable holds on his rank,
Unshaked of motion: and that I am he,
Let me a little show it, even in this;
That I am constant Cimber should be banish'd
And constant do remain to keep him so."

Bereft of all negative thoughts and attitudes, our minds are light and offer to become the springboards for our positive intentions and inclinations. In so doing, our minds are uplifted by our soaring spirits and we are enabled to transcend mental barriers and beyond where we will find our space to fulfill our cherished dreams without any let up. Like the balloon flying high above us, our fertile minds will also fly uninhibited with renewed zeal and greater conviction.

TWENTY-FIVE

STEPPING BACK

Karthik was glued to the TV. He was watching a wildlife programme on National Geographic channel. What had caught his attention was a tiger waiting in the shadows and watching a deer nibbling on some grass. The tiger was in no hurry to jump on his quarry and waited for the right moment when the deer was relatively off-guard. Then stepping back, the tiger took a massive lunge which caused it to land almost on top of the deer. Within seconds of a spirited chase, the deer had fallen prey to the tiger.

But a thought lingered in the ten-year-old lad's mind, which was 'why did the tiger step back before he jumped forward'? He went over to Vishwanath, his dad, who was reading the newspaper in the porch and posed him the question. His dad smiled at him and said, "Son, what you have just asked me is the basis of a great philosophy of achieving success in life. We are all trying to move forward all the time. We want to constantly advance in our careers, in our journey, in the discharge of our duties, etc. That's all okay and normal to feel so. But this rat race, as it is called, only results in a mad chase for money, material comforts, luxurious life, etc. without a thought whether we are actually going to possess these in our journey through life. In this relentless race, we may gather speed but we may lose our direction. We cannot be moving ahead like a herd of cattle goaded on by a cowherd. That would be disastrous. Instead, we need to chalk out or own paths like the tiger by having a clear perspective of our goal and the direction we need to take to achieve it. This is the reason that we need to step back, once in a while, to reflect and consider what progress we have achieved and what we need to do to continue on our path. This will allow us to have some breathing space and the opportunity to consolidate our strengths for a more directed effort."

Karthik smiled at his daddy and nodded his head in comprehension. Indeed, this was a great lesson that Vishwanath had imparted to his son, one which is at the very foundation of all progress.

History tells us that all forms of arduous human endeavour, necessitates stepping back from centre space in order to create a veritable springboard for effective and effortless action which leads to fruition with elan. Take the example of a trapeze artist in a circus. The artist holds on to the trapeze and then goes backwards and forwards to perform to everyone's exultation. Every time the artist goes backward, he or she gets the momentum necessary to swing ahead in the next instant. This is similar to the swing in a children's park. The swing, when brought backwards and then released, offers a wondrous experience to the child, who would then be able to swing back and forth for some time to come. A swimmer looking at the pool below from a springboard high above, will not take a plunge when he stands motionless on it. Instead, he will either depress the springboard with his legs to get the spring required to launch him for the somersaults before hitting the water or he would go back on the springboard and run in to gather momentum. Either way, he is 'stepping back' to move forward. Yet again, we have the case of a full back in football who, when confronted by two or three forwards of the rival team, would normally not try to dribble his way through. Instead, he would try and retrieve the ball and pass it backwards to the goalkeeper for safe collection, who would then kick the ball ahead into the centre field and thus thwart the immediate threat to the goal. And, of course, who can forget the strategy of guerilla warfare which, though on the path of silent extinction, often reminded us that it is necessary to step back and regroup when faced with reverses on the war front. In all the above cases, it is imperative to note that taking a step back in whatever way it is manifested, is not a sign of cowardice or regression but a strategy to renew one's effort towards one's objective.

Figuratively speaking, stepping back to step forward has been the at the very heart of our civilization. In one of the nuances of this concept, a marital relationship which may be on the rocks is often salvaged when one of the partners thereto, decides to step back and reflect on the ongoing tussle so as to evolve a workable solution for a lasting settlement of the vexatious issues that had caused the stalemate. In like manner, it would be masterly for an individual to walk away from an argument or a dispute which would be proving to be extremely sour if, in the individual's wiser judgement, it would be rational to maintain the relationship rather than break it.

This brings me to the all-important aspect of 'stepping back'. It prevents a souring relationship from tearing apart, it salvages a difficult situation which is on the point of breaking down, it brings to a naught the intransigence of a person and it helps in cooling off a simmering ego from venting anger. Nonetheless, it requires a herculean effort, a humble mind and a sincere temperament to 'step back' and effectively move on, for this is often construed by the arrogant, the inconsiderate, the immature and the argumentative individuals to be a sign of defeat. However, such individuals would be proved wrong by the subsequent events which would unfold to the benefit of the one who steps back. One step back does not bring defeat; it, in fact, rejuvenates you to make a wiser step forward in future.

TWENTY-SIX

EMOTIONAL ASPECT IN SUCCESS

A lot has been written about success, and opinions about its various connotations. True, that everyone yearns for success in life, whatever be their vocation or calling. But, is success all about trying to put in one's best endeavour, day in and day out, just to achieve the pinnacle from where one could view the vast landscape that was left behind in order to reach the top? That would make a person more like a mammon-mad mercenary, devoid of all emotions, concerns and empathy for his fellow human beings. Whether it is to do with working in the office, progressing in one's entrepreneurial venture or any other field of genuine individual growth, success would be bereft of its soul if it were to be divorced from its essential, emotional segment that ensures the individual remains grounded. That is why successful people are often those that take people along with them in their quest to reap their harvest and reach the zenith of their efforts.

Apart from this, there are two other aspects concerning success that are worth mentioning. One of these is that whatever you do, wherever you may be in your present status in life, try and *recollect all the good that others have done for you in your life* that would have helped you in one way or the other to steer clear of inconveniences, troubles or difficulties or simply feel good for having made your day. This is by no means an easy task. It would require you to sit down and systematically analyse, in a segmented format, your entire life till as far as you could possibly remember. Then, extremely methodically, you would need to jot down points on paper that remind you of the situations, that need not have been earth-shattering, but nevertheless were those that influenced your life at that point in time, even in a miniscule way, in which you received a kind word or a recommendation or any other form of help which lifted you from the relative depths of discomfort or loneliness to resettling your life and demeanour in a positive way. It would be ideal to assign those invigorating moments to specific individuals, so that at the end of your humongous exercise, you would have known where a particular individual stands in consonance with you in your journey through life. It matters not to enquire why the individual did what he did. What is material is to acknowledge the good or help that was imparted. Time will pass and with it the stories that were written on its sands, but memories would enlighten us to appreciate how our lives were influenced in a positive way by the multitude of people who crossed our path at some time or who were our co-passengers in the train journey of life. These memories will help us to focus on who are our genuine well-wishers and friends for we should not forget that 'a friend in need is a friend indeed'. When we are grateful for the good that we had received, we would be ever so humble to retain, in our memory, those moments in our lives.

A complementary quality that we need to possess in line with the above is that we should *not shove under the carpet all the wrongs that we may have done to others, inadvertently or otherwise.* This is indeed a difficult task to accomplish. It implies the availability of an inherent sense of integrity to acknowledge our dark side in our dealings with people around us. There may have been several situations in our lives when we had taken umbrage about things which didn't meet our expectations and admonished people for causing these to take place. Or, we may have brought misery to people around us for the erroneous decisions that we had taken, even without a specific intent to harm anyone. In either case, the consequences of our actions were tantamount to committing a wrongful deed in the lives of people who either depended on us or were, in some way or the other, instrumental in supporting us in our journey towards success. It may be true that at a specific point of time when such an incident transpired, it was necessary not to be guilty to the fault, for while the reprimand to a certain person or persons was required to instil discipline in adhering to a certain path, the error in the decision, as in the second case, was never intended, which, incidentally, is the principal ingredient which is supreme and not the action itself. Even so, it is necessary and the individual has a moral duty, maybe at a later stage in the other person's life, to show remorse not by apologizing or seeking forgiveness but by doing a good action, may be out of the blue, which would probably go to neutralize the effects of the erstwhile wrongful deed. In so doing, the individual would not only be showing empathy towards the other aggrieved person or persons, but would also bring solace to his own conscience, which would have constantly pricked him if he was righteous in his character.

Suffice it is, therefore, to mention that success is not entirely a focus on a cherished goal but the ability to arrive there with the confidence that we were grateful to those who helped us on our journey as well as empathetic to many who did not fall in line with our way of thinking.

TWENTY-SEVEN

Reclaim your Stage

Life is as mysterious as it is enjoyable. Every moment of each day brings with it its share of joy or sorrow, good tidings or foreboding ills. It has its ups and downs and in its wondrous dynamism is ensconced the numerous pulpits of human endeavour.

An individual, in his journey through life, traverses a multitude of situations which are often diverse in nature. His survival instinct deals with each situation in a manner that would ensure he emerges victorious from impending perils or succeeds over pitfalls that confront his path. Even so, it is well-nigh impossible for anyone to be always on the success trail.

Our lives are complex, however straightforward we may prefer to label it, in our urge to propound a theory that we are simple and unassuming people, more in the quest of ensuring that we lead reasonably comfortable lives than desperados who are battling it out in the rat race, on the other side of the hedge. We may be leading simple lives by our reckoning, but the relationships that we have nurtured or have been involved in, involuntarily or otherwise, in our intermingling with a variety of people from different backgrounds, cultures and skill sets would cause a perpetual intertwining of paths that create new vistas in honing our inter-personal skills.

This complexity in our lives is often the cause for encountering pitfalls that may deter us from proceeding unhindered in our journey towards our chosen goals. If we are unsuccessful in surmounting these hindrances, there is a possibility that we may be weaned away from the spotlight, for the present moment at least, till such time that the shadow of uncertainty has passed over our heads. Situations, such as these, often cause despondency and annoyance as the individual feels that the rhythm of his life has been upset. Consequently, there may be a tendency for the individual to withdraw into his shell from where he would be wont to create mountains of molehills, all to no avail.

It is the law of nature that precludes a person from being perpetually under the spotlight. In common parlance this is often stated as 'every day is not a Sunday'. If he were to languish in his present predicament and indulge in self-pity, he may never be able to emerge from the morass that he has fallen into and subsequently accentuated by his own making. A mature individual would use this sudden setback as an opportunity to introspect and analyse his flaws and shortcomings for chalking out a plan for course correction.

This is, therefore, the crux of the issue, namely that an inflexion point in a person's path towards his goal caused by a difficulty or shortcoming, is treated as a temporary aberration which could be easily overcome by reflecting upon the reasons for the same and creating a solution for the current problem as well as for similar problems in future. This would inherently require the person to 'depart' from the scene of action temporarily, only to return with reassurance and fortitude in having successfully calmed the storm.

Only a person with a fighting spirit would be able to accomplish this in his life, one who is undeterred by frequent bouts of failures, but, nevertheless, is successful in quelling a potentially vexatious issue or situation from aggravating to a point of no return. In doing so, he successfully reclaims his stage from where he had departed for a relatively short period. This is an important aspect that we need to imbibe in our daily lives, which is never to vacate for an extended duration, the platform on which we stand but to return with full force and confidence in having weathered the storm that, incidentally, had caused us to depart in the first place.

It would be foolhardy if a person decides to quit because of one setback where the situation would be analogous to him punching holes in all the remaining three tyres of his car just because the fourth tyre was flat. Coming back with a bang should be, therefore, the punchline in such situations, where the individual reclaims lost ground and stages a comeback which resurrects him securely, once again, in the path towards progress. This is the hallmark of a person with a 'never say die' attitude, one who is raring to have a go at whatever he was doing, all over again; like a famous saying goes, 'success lies not in never falling, but in rising every time we fall'.

TWENTY-EIGHT

Reach your Potential

A human being is born into a conservative mould. Everything he thinks or does, reflects his concern about not making a loss or mistake as the risk element in his life is kept subdued as being one low in priority. He has been intrinsically conditioned to act in this manner by the forces that pull him inwards to introspect on a particular situation or a given proposition. These are the subconscious mind and the nervous system within the individual.

These two principally dormant aspects of the human personality are responsible for engaging the individual in a perpetual tug-o-war with himself as to which decision he should take and why. They are springboards for extreme discretion and caution, and often are the basic cause for allowing anxiety within the self to flourish and gain ground. These two factors contribute to the human being becoming reticent to bell the cat whenever required and often goads the individual to take two steps backward rather than one step forward.

It, therefore, becomes an exercise of utmost necessity and importance to take stock of the influence of the subconscious and the nervous system in an individual's daily affairs and the harm that could be imparted to the person on account of the unbridled control exerted by these two elements in the life of an individual. Hence, the need of the hour would be to have the right perspectives in each situation and to systematically weed out the negative thoughts, beliefs and attitudes from one's mind, so that these do not ingress and lie buried in the domain of the subconscious.

Moreover, a person must try and reinvent himself by trying out something new and impressing others. In this manner, he would emerge from his cocoon which he had created around himself and evolve a vibrant personality, albeit involuntarily, which would form the mainstay for his future forays in his journey of life. It is by no means easy to do so for, while it satiates the feeling of the individual that he has completed his tasks within the framework of established rules, procedures and the law, it may not be lucrative for him to break out from his sequestered mindset and social compulsions, to go the extra mile.

And why should this be so difficult? Because, straying from the comfort zone which everyone has created for himself, though an act requiring gumption, will often lead to fear and panic as to the evolving consequences. But the plunge has to be taken if one needs to see light at the end of the tunnel. It is like the tale of the intrepid explorer who ventured into the unknown without a clue as to what lay ahead of him. He undergoes hardships, trials and tribulations, and finally, if and when he emerges victorious in his quest, he is able to signal to all the world that yet another milestone has been crossed and new vistas for development discovered.

To achieve this milestone, one needs to take spontaneous decisions. Continuous brooding and unproductive reflective behaviour could result in decadent thoughts leading to negative attitudes. In order to reach the full zenith of his potential, an individual must be ready to cast aside his cloak of pessimism and doubt, and forge ahead on his chosen path. There will be instances where fear and anxiety would creep in, but the individual who has built an abundant stock of self-confidence within himself would be able to take these in his stride, as he quells all opposition to his choice of the road not taken.

Reaching one's potential is important not only for the individual but for society as a whole. Just imagine the stock of human endeavour that would be created for all to mutually benefit if everyone were to strive to achieve the pinnacle of performance in his or her field of activity. Even the nation would progress at a fast past pace and be the beacon light in this world with its ever-increasing stories of darkness and misery. Self-motivation is an important tool to achieve one's potential as it inspires the individual to reach great heights which hitherto was conceived as being unattainable. There are, indeed, many paths we can take. We can choose to explore life with a spirit of adventure, or we can stay within a closed circle of comfort. It's not the place we live in, but our frame of mind that determines how far we go on our journey.

TWENTY-NINE

SETTING GOALS

In my earlier dispatch, I had dwelt on the concept of reaching one's potential by breaking all barriers. One of the principal ways of doing this is by setting goals for ourselves. Goal setting refers to that function to which our entire being is attuned, which focuses on the planning of steps and measures, bit by bit, in order to ensure that we attain the objectives in life that we have laid for ourselves within definite time frames. It is a carefully planned exercise which takes into account all the parameters that would otherwise influence the achievement of our goals as well as those that would facilitate the same.

There are several benefits of setting goals in life. Primarily, it provides a clear-cut direction for our lives, which would otherwise be lost in the milieu of distractions, failures, impulsiveness and misguided efforts. It sets out a lifestyle that one needs to adhere, to attain the otherwise difficult task of forging ahead on a chosen path. Besides, it also provides satisfaction to the individual as he progresses towards his goal in a directed manner rather than being jostled around like the seafarers in a rudderless craft. As it is said, 'if you fail to plan then you are planning to fail', so also setting goals in our lives gives us the confidence to concentrate our energies in a positive way. In so doing, we stay motivated towards achievement of our goals by being organized with clarity in our plan of action. Besides, goal setting helps one to be responsible and accountable to oneself by involuntarily honing one's skills of discipline, trouble-shooting, dedication and never-say-die attitude.

There are different types of goals, namely short-term, long-term, personal and professional. *Short-term* goals are those which are set for a relatively short timeframe, and the achievement of which go to help the work pertaining to the attainment of a larger goal. On the other hand, *long-term* goals refer to goals with a much longer timeframe for achievement and intrinsically require a more detailed plan and perseverance for attainment. While *personal* goals are those that are related to one's personal development, *professional* goals are those which are set to achieve objectives of one's job or enterprise.

It is important to adhere to a definite protocol for setting goals for achieving our objectives. First of all, one should have a *vision* of what one needs to achieve which, incidentally, should be realistic and achievable and then this is translated into a set plan of action called a *mission* which encompasses all those steps and procedures which would be instrumental in reaching the set goals. Along the way, there should be a provision for tracking one's progress and making correctional adjustments as required.

A mode of setting goals called SMART, is often employed by many enterprises and individuals to attain their objectives without much difficulty. SMART refers to *Specific, Measurable, Attainable, Relevant and Time-bound. Specific* refers to the aspect of clarity in setting goals where no avenue should be created for any sort of ambiguity. The goals which are set should be *measurable*, meaning thereby that the progress on the road to attainment of the goals should be capable of being easily tracked, and ambivalence, if any, should be nipped in the bud. Unrealistic goals may look good on paper but soon give rise to frustration and despondency on account of the inherent difficulties in achieving the same. Hence, goals should be plausible and *attainable*. It is, indeed, necessary to note that the goals should be *relevant* to the individual's line of activity or to an enterprise's business. Irrelevance leads to misguided and wasted efforts. For example, if a garment supplier is engaged solely in an online business, it would be infructuous for him to be devising goals for attainment of sales in brick-and-mortar stores. Finally, if goals are not *time-bound*, the aspect of seriousness in the whole exercise of goal setting would be lost and a lackadaisical attitude would step in, which would nullify all the genuine efforts that were undertaken to set the goals. Here, it would be pertinent to remember *Parkinson's law of delay* which states that 'work expands to fill in the time available for its completion'.

In conclusion, therefore, it may be said that goal setting and achievement of the same requires focus, dedication, motivation and conviction to cross all barriers and sail through towards progress.

THIRTY

GIVING BEGETS JOY

As Mahesh walked across the atrium of the shopping mall on his way out, he noticed an elderly couple just behind him. So, he opened the glass door and motioned to them with his outstretched hand that they could exit if they wanted to. The couple were pleasantly surprised at this show of etiquette from a stranger and obliged him by passing through the door and thanking him in the process. After they had gone, Mahesh felt a sense of happiness and well-being for having shown concern and care for the elderly couple.

Mahesh is not alone in this world to depict such small acts of kindness. Every day, millions of people go beyond the call of duty to extend that hand of help and care to their fellow human beings. These gestures enrich the lives of the giver in countless ways and brings about friendship and harmony in our relationships with total strangers. Besides, it provides a sense of fulfilment and purpose to the giver as well as happiness to the person receiving the care. This is what transpires when there is a display of concern from one human being to another.

Apart from this, of course, there is also the generous imparting of material gifts and benefits by one individual to another. For example, a man buys a bicycle to register his praise for his nephew who has fared well in his exams, or a girl buys a piece of jewellery to show her love for her mother on her birthday. These are tangible instances of care and concern which bring joy to the giver and happiness to the receiver.

It is important that such care and concern, whether it be material or otherwise, is shown with a genuine intent and purity of thought and is not vitiated by affectatious and hollow acts of 'kindness', which only go to satiate the Machiavellian designs of a dirty agenda. The individual who reaches out to another to extend some help or care must do so thoughtfully and be prepared to expend his resources in terms of time, energy and perhaps money. The soul of the act of giving that brings joy to the giver lies in this humble display of kindness without any thought or expectation of receiving some gift in return. Consequently, the giver needs to approach the entire act of kindness or concern from the pulpit of appreciation, gratitude and plenitude and not in any way display or exude that it was done to fulfil an obligation of an earlier act of help that was rendered.

Medically, the joy of giving brings about a lowering of blood pressure and strengthens the immune system. This translates to longevity in life spans as well as brings about decrease in the incidence of depression and anxiety.

Printed by Libri Plureos GmbH in Hamburg, Germany

9 798889 863496